You Can BEAT Those Spiritual BLAHS

Lew Miller

 ACCENT BOOKS
Denver, Colorado

ACCENT BOOKS
A Division of Accent-B/P Publications
12100 W. Sixth Avenue
P.O. Box 15337
Denver, Colorado 80215

Library of Congress Catalog Card Number: 78-72866

ISBN: 0-89636-015-6

Contents

This Thing Called "Revival"

Many Christians today live in perpetual defeat.

We worry and "go to pieces" just as if Christ did not live in us. Divorce and family miseries seem almost as prevalent among believers as in those who are without Christ. Our church work is often motivated by a sense of "oughtness" rather than by the overflow of a Spirit-controlled life.

Instead of living abundantly, so many of us merely exist, bent on "doing our own thing." Our churches quarrel, feud, and lull us to sleep. Many of us are on a starvation diet, for the Bible is virtually a closed Book in our lives—and often in our churches. Love and forgiveness are not practiced; therefore peace and joy are not possessed.

Is this a picture of *your* spiritual life? Such a picture is not healthy. Most Christians want something far better, and God certainly wants us to share His best.

The word *revival* has fallen into misuse, and now means many things to many people. To some evangelicals, it is synonymous with a scheduled period of evangelistic meetings, the major emphasis being to reach the lost. To others, *revival* denotes a time when everyone feels emotionally high. However, the word *revival* comes from two Latin words: *re,* meaning "again," and *vivo,* meaning "to live." When we talk about revival, we're talking about "living again." *Revival* means "to come alive." It can also be referred to as *renewal* — "to make new."

In its spiritual sense, revival or renewal is the abundant life each believer acquires when he allows the Lord Jesus to possess him fully. Christian revival can take place only as the work of Jesus Christ grips individual believers. It can never be promoted, scheduled, or structured.

It does not begin with unbelievers getting saved, but with believers getting right with God.

Our country's most desperate need is for a Heaven-sent, Holy Spirit-inspired, Bible-based revival that will transform Christian lives and churches to such an extent that unbelievers will be jealous of the victory they see in our Christian lives.

They will *see* the difference Christ makes, as He gives us peace instead of worry, calm instead of temper, joy instead of depression. They will note that we can live without horoscopes, drugs, and other forms of Satanism. They will see our homes become little bits of Heaven. They will see our churches in one accord—forgiving, loving, sharing, caring, reaching the lost.

Such revival life is what God has always intended for His children. For any Christian to live below these standards indicates a failure to accept all that God wants him to have.

For decades, churches have been striving to awaken Christians from their indifference, but meetings are often nothing more than religious vaudeville acts which excite people's emotions for a few days before they roll over and go back to sleep.

Such circuses would be amusing if they weren't so eternally poisonous. Since our church feels pressure to beat the neighboring church in the "numbers racket," it behooves us to put on a more spectacular show than they! We must invite the pink-and-green suited evangelist (with shoes to match), for his promise of fifty additions will outdo their yellow-suited evangelist with orange shoes who got only forty down the aisle. And our two-headed song leader will certainly compensate for their "busy little bees" program that drew seven busloads of kids and all the six-year-olds into the baptistry!

Such revivals build impressive statistical reports, but often they bring people into *church*-life rather than *Christ*-life. For a church to baptize anyone without seeing a clearcut testimony that the Lord Jesus now dwells within that person is a low form of hypocrisy. Such tactics may allow a church to lead a convention or conference in baptisms, but the real cheering is done by the hosts of Hell.

Perhaps the saddest note is that many pastors admit they can't find any converts two weeks later; yet, they continue scheduling extravaganzas in order to get their people "excited." Many of today's problems would be cured instantly if we followed Spurgeon's suggestion to "count the converts two years later." Many "converts" never are seen again after their baptism. True, there will always be those who fall away, but if we submit to God's methods, we will be enriched with fruit that remains.

As churches emphasize quantity instead of quality, using exaggerated means to get people down the aisle and into the baptistry, more harm than good is done to the cause of Christ. I fear for an old hound dog who might stray too close to a church building during a meeting. He's just liable to come out dripping wet!

The little Book of II Peter is "God's handbook for revival"! God's way of personal renewal is sane and right. Peter, writing under the inspiration of the Holy Spirit, gives us God's way, along with some warnings about that which is false. Too bad II Peter bears the reputation of being the most neglected book of the New Testament!

Twice Peter stated that his purpose for writing was to "stir up" God's people (1:13; 3:1). Just as people become physically tired and complacent, Christians often become spiritually lethargic and need to be aroused — stirred up. Peter's reason for writing, then, was to awaken believers to spiritual vitality. The term *stir up* means to revive, and so in this brief epistle we can learn how to be revived. Of course, any Christian bookstore has dozens of books on the subject, but II Peter is different. It is autographed by God. It is His Word, the only authentic handbook on revival.

You, the reader, are about to embark on a spiritual adventure. You're going to discover just how simple, yet dynamic, God's prescription for spiritual vitality really is.

If your faith has been in doldrums recently, and if you desire a closer, more intimate, more fulfilling walk with the Lord, then it is my prayer that the principles for such daily victory leap from these pages into your heart... and enrich your life to the fullest!

Lew Miller
Tequesta, Florida

1
The Great Swap

*I*n 1970, I was assigned as a foreign missionary to build an English language church in Taichung, Taiwan. Having served previously as the first pastor of each of three fast-growing Baptist missions, I was confident that in a matter of time I would build a successful church overseas.

Sure enough, starting with twenty-six members, it took me only seven months to build the church—all the way down to fifteen attenders! For the first time in my Christian professional life, I cratered! Disappointed, disillusioned, and despairing, I found no glamour in foreign missions work. My first seven months were a spiritual nightmare.

I could think of nothing but quitting or, at the very least, trying to get a more sensible assignment. I requested a transfer, but our mission representative, knowing the complete assurance we had felt in the Lord's guidance to Taiwan, urged me to stay a little longer.

Three weeks later, "my" congregation of 15 had become 106. Four months after that, we reached the 300 mark and stayed there. Those remaining three years in Taiwan became the best years of my life.

What accounted for this transformation? While waiting for my transfer, I studied the life of another troubled missionary, the Apostle Paul. I reasoned that if I could learn the secret of his abundant life, there might be hope for me.

I was at first amazed by Paul's estimate of himself, ". . . though I be nothing" (II Corinthians 12:11). He restated this theme, ". . . if a man think himself to be something, when he is nothing, he deceiveth himself" (Galatians 6:3). But his "nothingness" did not bring self-pity or depression. Instead, he found victory by looking *outside* himself to the One who is everything, Jesus Christ. Paul let another live his life for him. "Not I, but Christ liveth in me" (Galatians 2:20b).

Paul gave up trying to live the Christian life, for he knew *he* couldn't do it successfully. Instead, he allowed Jesus Christ, the only One who *can* live the Christian life, to be his life. He "swapped out" Paul for Christ and became the most powerful Christian of all time.

At first, this Bible teaching really discouraged me. During my seventeen years as a Christian, I had faithfully studied and memorized Scripture, but realize now I knew little about *practical* Christian living. My study provided theory—I knew Jesus as Lord, and I had certainty about my salvation. But, while I had tried my best to live victoriously, my missionary trip to Taiwan had shown me how totally incapable I was of grasping the "victorious Christian life."

MY SEARCH FOR MEANING

For the first twenty-two years of my life, I had tried almost everything known to man in order to get right with God. As a baby, I had been sprinkled; at twelve, I was confirmed. During high school and college, I had tried membership in two different denominations. Then I professed atheism for several years. I even tried to find peace from my intense fear of death by turning to reincarnation.

A piece of paper called a college diploma provided no

indication that I had found any sound answers to my seekings. At twenty-two, I was empty and purposeless. I had tried everything I could to improve my life and nothing had worked.

After one disastrous year in the Air Force, I was assigned to room with a man who lived and loved the Lord Jesus. This didn't make me too happy, for he felt he should share his faith with his roommate. I tried to stop him, but I knew I was licked when I offered unsuccessfully to exchange roommates with every man in my squadron!

Jim repeatedly told me that God had the answer for my miserable life—the gift of His Son, Jesus Christ. By sneaking looks into Jim's Bible, which he had "accidentally" left by my bed, I learned that God had already dealt with the only real problem I had—sin. God began to deal personally with me through His Word. Although I did not hear audible voices, the exchange went something like this:

> *God:* Miller, you are a mess. Aren't you going to do anything about it?
> *Miller:* I've tried everything I can think of. Nothing works for me.
> *God:* I'd like to do something for you.
> *Miller:* What do you have in mind?
> *God:* I want to make a swap with you.
> *Miller:* A swap? What do you want to trade?
> *God:* I'd like to swap My Son for your sin.

Just imagine! God wanted me to give Him my sin problem. In turn, He would send His Son to live in me! Instead of swapping out immediately, I spent several frustrating months arguing with God and defending my religion and ideas to Jim. Finally, one day by faith, I agreed to the swap. I gave my heart and life to Jesus Christ. My sin was forgiven, and I began a new life.

This swap is Biblical. Paul stated: "For he [God] hath

made him [Christ] to be sin for us, who knew no sin; that we might be made the righteousness of God in him" (II Corinthians 5:21). But there is more to victorious living than just receiving the Lord Jesus.

As faithful as my friends were in telling me how to become a Christian, they did not tell me of the day-by-day practical Christian walk. Neither did my Bible college professors. And I didn't hear a single word about it in seminary. For seventeen years I struggled to live victoriously, failing to heed the simple admonition: "As ye have therefore received Christ Jesus the Lord, so walk ye in him" (Colossians 2:6).

Many times I had heard preachers tell of the importance of receiving the Lord Jesus. I myself had preached this marvelous gospel thousands of times; however, I had never heard a Bible message on the practical, abundant Christian life.

My own treatment of this subject was theoretical. I had a practical salvation that took care of my sin, death, and Hell; yet, I was struggling frantically to experience day-by-day victory. I needed something that worked in my home, on the job, and everywhere I went. Couldn't the God who did such a masterful job of assuring my eternity do something about my daily walk in this world?

Certainly I had heard "psychological" sermons on how to live victoriously. "Try your best to be like Jesus," "Give of your best to the Master," "Try harder," "Do more for Jesus," "Keep struggling until you gain the victory," and "Attend more meetings." Nothing could be more impractical and unbiblical than these sermons I heard—and preached—about successful Christian living.

THE SECRET OF SUCCESS

In studying Paul, I noticed a complete absence of do-it-yourself techniques. Paul wasn't trying to live the

Christian life! He wasn't doing his best! He wasn't trying to do things for Jesus! As a spiritual nothing, he realized it was useless to strive for victory. From my study of Paul's life, I discovered that *the Christian life is not hard to live. It is impossible!* Paul couldn't live it; you can't live it; I can't live it; and God never tells us to try. So it is futile for me to try my best to do the impossible!

A companion truth also became evident: *There is one person—and only one—who has ever lived up to God's standard: Jesus Christ!* For thirty-three years, Jesus Christ proved He could do it. And now, I realized as I studied more, He is living in me, making His resurrection power available to me. No longer was He simply an historical Christ, nor was He distant. He was living in me.

Do-it-yourself programs hinder spiritual progress. What a relief it was to me to learn that God had not sent me to Taiwan to build a church! My church-building reputation was not at stake, for a "nothing" has no reputation. I needed only to trust the indwelling Christ with each day's problems and live in vital union with Him. All He wanted was a clean channel through whom He could work. It was up to *Him* to build that church. So, again, I swapped out. I swapped out all my failures for His success. He would do what I was unable to do.

As I began to experience victory in Christ, my preaching took on a new dimension, and so did our church. We lost interest in statistics. People became more important than numbers. We discovered that a church could carry on an effective Bible-teaching program without counting attendance or professions of faith. We were living witnesses that Biblical Christianity works just as well in the twentieth century as it did in the first.

We learned the joy of participating in a simple, unstructured program of Bible study and evangelism, instead of the high-geared rat race that many churches promote. A holy excitement developed as we studied God's

14

Word and witnessed life-changing, home-saving victories on a day-by-day basis. Fellowship was the sweetest I'd ever known!

As we experienced the joy of being filled with the Spirit of Christ, friends began to notice the difference in our lives. Because the vacuum in us had been filled by Jesus, we had practical answers for fellow strugglers. Jesus Christ became the solution to home and marital problems. His power and Spirit cut across denominational and national lines, converting and enveloping in one fellowship Americans, Chinese, Europeans, Australians; former Black Muslims, Satanists, Roman Catholics, Jews, and Buddhists.

We found freedom in renting a building on Sundays and Wednesdays rather than building our own, though building money was available. Renting eliminated many time-consuming housekeeping chores and enabled us to have more time for ministry. Even more important, it took Christianity out of the church building and onto the air base or wherever our members went.

After experiencing such revival in Taiwan, I know that "swapping out" works. Our fatality rate after the first six years was small. Most of these young Christians are today moving toward spiritual maturity. Few have fallen away.

This undignified, non-theological term, *swapping out,* has been used to lead a great number of Christians into such a victorious life. While the term admittedly is not for academic use, it describes exactly what each of us must do to beat those spiritual blahs. Swapping out sin for salvation is something lost friends can understand, and swapping out carnal defeat for spiritual victory provides a simple entrance into abundant living for the believer. Swapping out is a term people seem to grasp when more noble theological terms alienate them. It is really a synonym for the kind of revival the Bible teaches.

YOU CAN BEAT THOSE SPIRITUAL BLAHS

In the following pages, as we examine the second letter of the Apostle Peter, you will see how you can apply this exciting concept in your own life to realize the full joy of your walk with God.

16

2
Two Keys To Spiritual Vitality

*I*magine the excitement among the early believers when they learned that another letter had arrived from the apostle! His first epistle had been such encouragement to these suffering Christians. Picture their enthusiasm as they impatiently open this second scroll to learn "what's new." Then, with a tinge of disappointment, they read: "Nothing new—just my funeral announcement and a few exhortations before I depart."

Second Peter is the apostle's swan song, his dying words. Jesus had promised that Peter would die a violent death which would glorify God (John 21:18, 19). Now, in his old age, Peter calmly faced this martyrdom. Tradition declares that, shortly after writing this epistle, he was hanged upside down on a cross.

In light of the impending tragedy, we should expect to read of tension and fears. Instead, Peter calmly described his Christian death as 'folding up his tent.' His only concern was for the spiritual condition of the churches he was leaving behind (1:15). He wanted God's people to live in victory, so his letter dealt with abundant life, not death.

The theme of his message: *Stirring up God's people through the process of swapping out their lives with the Lord Jesus.*

> *Simon Peter, a servant and an apostle of Jesus Christ, to them that have obtained like precious faith with us through the righteousness of God*

and our Saviour Jesus Christ (1:1).

Years ago, on an old camping ground in Massachusetts, Dr. Charles J. Erdman of Princeton Theological Seminary announced that his subject for the evening was "Simon Johnson of Fishtown." The audience was shocked until he finished his statement by saying, "alias St. Peter the Rock."

He then proceeded to point out that Simon Johnson of Fishtown was just an ordinary fellow with an ordinary name, but one in whom the Lord Jesus did a terrific job. Simon, son of John (Johnson), came from Bethsaida (Fishtown), so Simon Johnson of Fishtown became Peter the Rock.

Simon was the name given him at birth; *Peter* was the name given him by the Lord at his new birth. *Simon* speaks of the old, unregenerate man before he came to know and serve the Lord; *Peter* speaks of the new man, transformed by the grace of God.

Peter was one of the inner circle of Jesus' disciples. An impetuous, headstrong fisherman, he was a man of great passion. When he leaped into the sea to meet his Lord, he walked on the water for a little while. He uttered the sublime confession of faith concerning Jesus: "Thou art the Christ, the Son of the living God" (Matthew 16:16). He desired the tabernacles to be constructed on the Mount of Transfiguration. He denied the Lord under pressure and was subsequently forgiven. He rushed to Jesus' tomb and was the first to enter it. He was spokesman for the early church, the speaker on the Day of Pentecost, and the one who opened the way for Gentiles to receive the gospel.

GLORIOUS SERVITUDE

This famous Christian, whom some call the first pope,

identified himself as a bondslave. He acknowledged that he did not belong to himself, but was possessed completely by the Lord Jesus Christ who purchased him with His shed blood at Calvary.

A slave always disregards his interests and does what his master commands. Likewise, a Christian must disregard his interests and put himself at the Lord's disposal. This is exactly what Peter did, and he discovered that there is no greater place of joy. Willing servitude to the Lord is real, meaningful living.

This same note of lordship needs to be sounded in our evangelism efforts. It is neither fair nor Biblical to let people think they can get to Heaven by receiving Jesus as Saviour without giving Him claim on their lives. Salvation requires a change of ownership. Jesus Christ moves in and takes over as Lord (Boss!); thus, upon receiving Him into our lives, we no longer have rights of our own.

God bases the salvation He offers on the lordship of Jesus Christ. When the jailer asked what he had to do to be saved, Paul answered, "Believe on the Lord Jesus Christ, and thou shalt be saved" (Acts 16:31b). When Paul wrote to the Romans regarding the way of salvation, he said, "That if thou shalt confess with thy mouth the Lord Jesus, and shalt believe in thine heart that God hath raised him from the dead, thou shalt be saved" (Romans 10:9).

When Peter preached to the multitudes on the Day of Pentecost, his plea was, "Whosoever shall call on the name of the Lord shall be saved" (Acts 2:21b). The Bible message to the lost is consistent. If Jesus is to be your Saviour, He must be *Lord* of your life.

When you receive Jesus Christ as Saviour, He *purchases* you, becomes your owner. Paul wrote: "What? know ye not that your body is the temple of the Holy Ghost [Spirit] which is in you, which ye have of God, and *ye are not your own?* For ye are bought with a price: therefore glorify God with your body, and in your spirit, *which are God's*" (I Corinthians 6:19, 20; italics mine).

The Bible says not a single word about a salvation which takes us to Heaven when we die but allows us to be lord of our life on earth. Many people have been deluded into eternal Hell by relying on a kind of salvation which God does not offer.

Peter called himself a bondslave, but don't feel sorry for him! Being a bondslave, in love, to Jesus Christ is better than being pope! How much better this "slavery" than a self-styled life! Peter was impulsive, hot-tempered, proud, unsteady, and boastful of his own ways. But, like Christians today who rejoice in willing servitude to the Lord, Peter had a much better life when he submitted his ways to the Lord. He learned the better way of swapping out with Jesus.

DIVINE CALLING

Peter was also an apostle, but not because he ran for the office or appointed himself. This was the Lord's gift to His bondslave. God has a similar place of service for each of His children, and life's greatest joy comes from serving in this capacity.

Peter's apostleship authenticated his message. When he tells us how to have personal revival, we really ought to perk up our ears, for in reality we are learning what God says. It's tragic when we get so busy mapping out our own strategy that we miss God's authentic way.

PETER'S MAILING LIST

The risen Christ personally commissioned the apostle to feed and shepherd the sheep and lambs of His flock. In both of his epistles, Peter addressed himself to those persecuted sheep of the house of Israel who were dispersed among all nations. His first epistle offered encouragement to those scattered Jews to patiently trust in the Lord, even in the midst of their suffering.

His second epistle has a broader outreach. It has fewer Jewish overtones and is addressed to all believing Gentiles as well as Hebrew Christians. His mailing list includes all who share his faith in the Lord Jesus. This faith is the difference between the Christian gospel and every other religion or religious system. It is not attained by works or human effort, but by grace. Man says "attain"; God says "obtain." It is most important to determine the basis upon which *your* hope rests.

Precious faith is available "through the righteousness of our God, Jesus Christ, and our Saviour, Jesus Christ" (II Peter 1:1b; literal translation). Contrary to the teachings of every cult, Jesus Christ is God. God is our Saviour! He suffered all the torments of Hell on the cross, not as punishment for His sins (He had none), but as full punishment for ours. "Who his own self bare [archaic tense: *bore*] our sins in his own body on the tree, that we, being dead to sins, should live unto righteousness: by whose stripes ye were healed" (I Peter 2:24).

Christ died the sinner's death, but He came alive again—victor over sin, death, and the grave. We obtain precious faith by believing this gospel account, which involves acknowledging our wretched sinfulness and receiving the living Lord into our lives.

We need not, in fact we cannot, add to the gospel masterpiece. Christ's death serves as full payment for our sins; His burial takes care of our cemetery problems; and His resurrection provides a living Lord for every believer. He is all we need—now and forever!

SALUTATION: THE GREATEST BLESSING THIS SIDE OF HEAVEN

*Grace and peace be multiplied unto you through
the knowledge of God, and of Jesus our Lord (1:2)*

Even a common greeting cannot be ignored in God's Word. Peter prayed that, as a result of heart knowledge of "our God, even Jesus the Lord" (literal translation), we will experience increasing grace and peace in our lives. The more intimate our relationship with Him, the greater our experience of grace (living on the resources of God) and peace (living in the security of God).

Notice that we do not *develop* grace and peace in our lives; we *receive* them! In fact, we swap out our miseries and insecurities for them. Both grace and peace are multiplied as we yield to the Lord's control.

Even the order of the two words is significant. A search for peace must be preceded by a quest for God's grace. Until we live on the resources of Christ, we cannot know His abiding peace. Life's greatest blessing—God's smile resting upon us and God's peace filling our hearts—is only experienced by knowing the Lord Jesus personally and intimately.

THE HEART OF REVIVAL TEACHING

Second Peter 1:3-4 are the key verses of this epistle and make up one of the greatest passages of the New Testament. Wanting to stir up revival, Peter points out two rich blessings which come from knowing the Lord Jesus personally and intimately. These blessings, divine power and precious promises, are God's two keys to an abundant life of victory.

KEY ONE: THE BLESSING OF DIVINE POWER

> *According as his divine power hath given unto*
> *us all things that pertain unto life and godliness,*
> *through the knowledge of him that hath called us*
> *to glory and virtue (1:3).*

This verse contains the heart of the Christian message, neglected truths which the Christian world desperately needs to hear. It lays the axe to much false teaching about the Christian life and shows that we don't need anything but Jesus Christ.

A Christian is what he is, not because of what he does, but because of what he receives!

Man is unable to save himself or to live the Christian life in his own strength, but all God's power is available and ready to be used in the two areas with which we are most concerned: life (what we do) and godliness (what we are).

No man can save himself, so spiritual life must be received as a gift from God which comes through knowing the Lord Jesus. "For the wages of sin is death, but the gift of God is eternal life through Jesus Christ our Lord" (Romans 6:23). Ninety-two New Testament passages define salvation as a gift from God. His divine power gives us all things that pertain to life. We don't have what it takes, but God provides for our insufficiencies.

In like manner, the daily, practical Christian life is also a gift from God, one that comes from knowing intimately the indwelling Lord Jesus. His divine power furnishes all things that pertain to godliness.

The tense of the Greek word *given,* which here denotes "large-handed generosity," is significant. It shows that God in one past act has given us every spiritual blessing, with the results coming in the present.

When a person is born again, the Holy Spirit takes up

residency in his body. Since the Holy Spirit is a person, He does not come to us in installments. At the moment of conversion, we receive all the Holy Spirit we're ever going to get, and He promises never to leave us or forsake us (Hebrews 13:5). No need to chase around looking for "more of the Spirit" or a "second blessing" or any particular spiritual gift. Paul tells us that "... the God and Father of our Lord Jesus Christ ... hath blessed us [past] tense, *once and for all*] with all spiritual blessings in heavenly places [that refers to victory life here and now] in Christ" (Ephesians 1:3).

When we have received salvation in the Lord Jesus Christ, we have all the blessings and gifts we're getting because Jesus Christ is all we need. He brings the total wealth of Heaven to our lives. The Holy Spirit brings us growth and victory by making Jesus real to us, but He does not add to the blessings we have in Christ. He doesn't have to! We are *complete in Christ,* who is the "head of all principality and power" (Colossians 2:10b), and one cannot be more complete!

All that pertains to life and godliness is given us when we receive the Lord Jesus into our lives. We need only discover and develop the resources we already have. We need not live as paupers, for the King with all His possessions lives within us! The full potential for abundant life dwells within each Christian. Victory comes as we appropriate it.

Before returning from Taiwan to begin what later proved to be two hundred thousand miles of travel in Bible conference ministry, I was overwhelmed by a gift from an Air Force officer. Rich gave me two major oil company credit cards with power of attorney to use them for any needs up to one thousand dollars a month. Never had I experienced such generosity—or so I thought at the time. However, when the cards expired a year later, I had spent only $7.80 (and that bailed me out of a real emergency).

Why didn't I use them more? As gracious and generous as Rich had been, he was too late! A previous Benefactor had already promised to supply all my needs "according to his riches in glory by Christ Jesus" (Philippians 4:19).

Of course, He often uses people like Rich, but, in this case, He used other means. Income was incredibly low for supporting a wife and four teenagers. Repeatedly, unsolicited money came from unusual sources just in the nick of time. All bills were paid on schedule although we rarely knew the day before how they would be taken care of. But I couldn't honestly use Rich's credit cards because there were no legitimate needs.

God's "credit cards" drawn on the Bank of Heaven provide so much more than financial and material needs only—love, joy, peace, longsuffering, gentleness, goodness, faith, meekness, and temperance. Horatius Bonar, a godly preacher of the past, stated it well: "Believers are not hired servants supporting themselves by their own works, but children maintained at their Father's expense."

KEY TWO: THE BLESSING OF PRECIOUS PROMISES

Whereby are given unto us exceeding great and precious promises: that by these ye might be partakers of the divine nature, having escaped the corruption that is in the world through lust (1:4).

Along with God's divine power, we are also granted hundreds, even thousands, of wonderful promises from God. Through these, we become partakers of the divine nature and escape the corruption and slavery resulting from lust. In fact, the entire Christian faith is based upon God's promises. They are the essence of the spiritual life.

The word *partakers* means "to become a part and have something become a part of you." By appropriating the provisions contained in the promises of the Word, believers share the character of God—both his excellency and His glory. This is what it means to be born again.

Christ in us is the source of our supply, the fulfillment of all the Bible promises. All the desires and ambitions of a man find their fulfillment in Him. Paul says that in Christ all the promises of God are "yea! and Amen!" When we come in touch with the Lord Jesus, we move in to a new way of life because we share His nature. In Him, we find the power to cope with the corruption of the world. By knowing Him personally, we share the life of God. Since He is Master of every circumstance and knows what to do in every situation, we can experience day-by-day victory by drawing on His resources.

In other words, we swap out all that we are not and cannot do for all that the indwelling Christ is and can do through us! And His resources are made known to us through Bible promises.

God, the great Giver, has supplied promises to meet every need in the lives of His children. We do not need to give way to worry, fear, or defeat, for the Adequate One dwells within. We do not lack wisdom or knowledge, for the indwelling Christ has a corner on the market. We need not hate people, lose our tempers, gossip, or commit adultery, for the Overcomer lives in us. Because Christ in us is our hope of glory, we can live in peace, joy, and certainty. There is no area in any Christian's life which is not covered by a promise from the Father, and the promises are as strong as the Promiser!

One of the simplest, yet most inspiring, forms of Bible study is to search the Word for the promises of God. You won't have to look hard; they are on every page! Divide a sheet of paper into three columns, and list each promise in the first column. The second column should be headed

"Conditions." In it, list any qualifications the Bible makes for claiming the promise. Some promises are conditional; others are unconditional.

For example, Isaiah 26:3 is conditional: "Thou wilt keep him in perfect peace, whose mind is stayed on thee: because he trusteth in thee." The promise is perfect peace. However, the qualification for receiving this peace involves focusing our minds on the Lord and trusting in Him. By contrast, Hebrews 13:5b is unconditional. It requires no action by the believer. God says, "I will never leave thee, nor forsake thee." The promise is His continual presence, and there are no qualifications.

The third column, an important one, is headed, "What I Have Done About This Promise." Filling in this column makes your Bible study personal and challenging. You will begin to realize that you are stumbling and living in misery because you have not appropriated the promised blessings.

You will begin to experience joy and victory as you trust God more. I have seen a Bible study group continue for several weeks on just this simple but thrilling format. It works well for private devotions, too.

THE PROMISE	CONDITIONS TO BE MET	WHAT I HAVE DONE ABOUT THIS PROMISE
Eternal life John 3:16	*Believe in Him*	*Received Him as my Saviour and Lord*
Perfect peace Isaiah 26:3	*Mind stayed on the Lord; trust in Him.*	*Making some progress. Prone to look at the problem instead of Him.*
His abiding presence Hebrews 13:5	*Unconditional*	*I rest in the security I've found in Him.*

Forgiveness and cleansing *I John 1:9*	*Confess my sins, agreeing with God about them.*	*Am progressing in this area, finding it easier to confess my sins—and gaining victory over my guilt feelings.*
Success *Joshua 1:8*	*Meditating on the Word, doing what It says.*	*Must spend more time in the Word; need more devotional time.*
His Return *John 14:2, 3*	*Unconditional*	*Wait for Him and prepare. No longer scares me.*

The promises are inexhaustible! You'll never run out! Here are a few more to get you started:

His presence—Isaiah 41:10
Help in temptation—
  Hebrews 4:16
Promotion—Psalm 75:6, 7
Forgiveness—Psalm 86:5
Strength—Isaiah 40:31
Guidance—Proverbs 3:6
Courage—Psalm 27:14

Fruitfulness—II Peter 1:8
Prosperity—Psalm 1:2, 3
Instruction—John 16:13
Provision—Philippians 4:19
Answered prayer—Matthew 7:7
Protection—Psalm 34:7
Help in trouble—Psalm 50:15

Remember, by claiming the promises of God we become "partakers of the divine nature, having escaped the corruption that is in the world through lust." Search for those promises. Meet the conditions. Every condition will prove to be an added blessing. Then honestly report your personal progress in each area.

Can you see God's way of revival unfolding? His power supplies everything we need for salvation, the gift of life, and for Christian living, the gift of godliness. Many evangelical churches do a great job teaching the truth of salvation, that it is all God's work; then do an inadequate job teaching about the Christian life, implying that it's all up to us.

Truly believing that God gives *all things* that pertain to *life* will put an end to the ridiculous gimmicks and pressures that drag people into the baptistry. Truly believing that God gives *all things* that pertain to *godliness* will put an end to do-it-yourself programs for Christian living. How fortunate the person who, learning that he can neither save himself nor live the Christian life, turns both his hope of eternal life and his desire for abundant life over to the Lord Jesus! Swapping out with Jesus for all the promised blessings really works!

Second Peter 1:12-15 shares the secret of God's revival victory. Though flesh ministries continually look for something new, Peter stressed that it is through remembering the old that Christians keep their faith alive and vital. Four times he used the word *remembrance* in describing how to stir up believers (1:12, 13, 15; 3:1).

While many clamor for something new, unusual, or sensational, the apostle admonishes us to re-emphasize old truths. To his dying day, he attempted to stimulate believers with a holy zeal and a concern for souls by continually reiterating the fundamentals of the faith.

He did not mention stirring up the church by bringing in the ex-dope addict or the movie star or rock musicians. Such entertaining often stirs up the wrong part of us—the flesh! On the other hand, Bible truths speak to the total person and bring about lasting changes.

Since Peter makes *remembrance* the key to spiritual rejuvenation, it is imperative that he tell us just what to remember. He used the phrase *these things* five times (1:8, 9, 10, 12, 15), referring to the foundational truths of the Scriptures, truths which must be remembered if we are to win over spiritual depression. More specifically, they are the seven qualities with which every Christian is to be equipped (1:5-7):

virtue
knowledge
temperance
patience
godliness
brotherly kindness
love

These are the great qualities—all supplied through Bible promises—that bring fullness of joy and fruitfulness of life. They are essential for a revived life or a revived church. They are the truths upon which abundant life is based, characteristics every Christian should evidence in his faith.

If *these things* are in you and overflowing, you will be an effective and fruitful Christian (1:8).

If you lack *these things,* you will be a carnal, defeated Christian, full of doubts and troubles (1:9).

If you do *these things,* you will not stumble through the Christian life (1:10).

If you know *these things,* you will be established in the truth (1:12).

These things are the revival truths Peter wanted us to remember after his departure (1:15).

Putting Peter's key terms together, we can formulate God's Prescription for Revival:

　　Remembrance (1:12, 13, 15; 3:1)
　　　　of these things (1:8, 9, 10, 12, 15)
　　　　　　= *stirring up* (*revival!*) (1:13; 3:1).

Revivals must be founded, not on sensational new truths or methods, but on constant emphasis on old truth. We don't need anything new. We don't need revival strategy or gimmicks. We need verse-by-verse teaching of the Word of God! We must have the foundational truths of God brought to mind again and again.

Peter, in describing this way of real renewal, declared

that the power of God has provided all that is necessary to live life at its fullest. By His glorious power, God has called us, given us a knowledge of Christ, and bestowed upon us wonderful promises. By means of His divine power and precious promises He is working in believers in such a way as to produce new ambitions, appetites, and actions. By partaking of the new nature He gives us, we have everything necessary for living a godly life.

RESPONDING TO GOD'S REVIVAL PLAN

And beside this, giving all diligence, add to your faith virtue; and to virtue knowledge (1:5).

"And beside this" is better translated, "for this very reason." Because we have experienced the new birth and because this knowledge of the Lord Jesus provides us with His power and promises, we cannot sit back and be content with saving faith only. It is ultra-important for each Christian to see that these seven graces are included in life. Otherwise, Christianity may be a "ticket to Heaven," but it will be dull, boring, and unfruitful on the way there—and also a poor testimony to unbelievers.

"[For this very reason], giving all diligence, add to your faith . . . ." Spiritual life will not take place automatically or accidentally. Peter urged us to hasten with all diligence to cooperate with the Spirit of God in developing these beautiful graces. The divine nature we receive when we become Christians does not automatically produce a rich life. We must live in dependence upon the resources God has planted within us, claiming all the promises of the Book. A lazy, indifferent believer will go nowhere, except to Heaven!

Add means to supplement your faith, building a superstructure on the foundation of saving faith. From the picturesque Greek word we get our English word *choreography*. It implies putting all these graces together in harmony, supplying one quality to another.

We do not add these characteristics one at a time as the wording of the King James Version appears to teach. Virtue, knowledge, temperance, and so on are not separate, detached entities, each of which could be tied or stuck on to the others. Properly translated, "supply within your faith virtue" means that these qualities are not disjointed or disconnected. They describe a Christlike life. All are readily available to every believer through the indwelling Christ as soon as we claim them by faith.

Remember, God has given us all things that pertain to life and godliness. Therefore, these seven graces which bring abundant life are gifts to be received. They are not rewards for hard work. The true idea of "giving all diligence" is that you hasten with real eagerness to receive all that God has for you.

For decades, Christians have lived in defeat because they have tried to work hard to be good. One modern paraphrase even comes right out and says in verse 5 that we must work hard to obtain these gifts. But the context of this passage reveals that just the opposite is true. If you want to crater in Christian living, just try to work hard to be good. Be assured of failure before you start! How can you work for a gift? If you earn something, then it isn't a gift at all. The truth is that Jesus Christ *is* each one of these graces that we must add to our faith. He is virtue! He is knowledge! He is love! And because He lives in me, all these traits are mine if I appropriate His life—or swap out for them.

Peter had no thought of the time-sequence in which these virtues appear. He set them before us in the order of their natural relationship. Each acts upon all, and all commence simultaneously. Love is at the end of the list, virtue at the beginning; yet, they were born at the same hour. One need not wait for the first six graces before he or she can experience love.

Faith in the Lord Jesus Christ—the foundation for all spiritual growth and service—is the root from which all these graces spring.

3
The Seven Traits
Of A
Growing Life

*T*he faith that saves is the foundation for the full Christian life and mature Christian character. What can happen to our faith when we supplement it with the seven character traits of Christ?

> *And beside this, giving all diligence, add to your faith virtue; and to virtue knowledge; and to knowledge temperance; and to temperance patience; and to patience godliness; and to godliness brotherly kindness; and to brotherly kindness charity [love] (1:5-7).*

THE FIRST TRAIT: VIRTUE

Scholars have a difficult time defining *virtue.* It means excellence, and also courage. Sometimes it is translated *manliness.* It is a moral strength and purity which includes winning the battle of the mind against physical lust.

Perhaps the expression *spiritual tone* comes closest to describing this trait which needs to be developed in Christians. In athletics, the term *muscle tone* is used to describe one whose muscles are responsive and can move properly on command. Spiritual tone is that quality of life which enables us to respond immediately when God speaks. Swiftly we move in whatever direction the Holy

Spirit guides.

This ability comes only when we yield fully as commanded by Paul, "I beseech you therefore, brethren, by the mercies of God, that ye present your bodies a living sacrifice" (Romans 12:1a). The tense of the Greek verb calls for a once-and-for-all presentation of our bodies to God. Many believers stop at this point. Somehow we have the idea that we should present various areas of our lives to God, one by one. This year we give Him our money, next year our family life, then our children, next our time, then our talents. This is not God's way. He does not ask for separate compartments of our lives. He asks for only one thing, bodies, in a complete and final transaction.

Until this exchange takes place, there will be no Christian victory because there has been no obedience. Yielding our bodies as living sacrifices should take place at the moment of conversion. If it was neglected then, it becomes our next item of business with God.

This presentation of our bodies to God does not mean we will never sin nor stumble. It simply means that we give up all rights to self so that Christ can live in us and make us spiritually sharp. It shows, too, that the Lord will never settle for less than one hundred percent. If He is not Lord of all, He is not Lord at all.

This is reasonable service, true even in human relationships. What reaction could be expected if a husband told his wife that he was eighty percent faithful to her? In Old Testament times, when a priest was consecrated, he was covered with the anointing oil from head to foot. God's requirements have not changed. He still insists on a once-and-for-all yielding of the whole body.

At this point, an abuse exists in our modern-day "revivals." People are called upon to "rededicate" their lives. With many, this has become almost a ritual. Every spring and every fall, well-intentioned people go forward and rededicate themselves, hoping for something better in their Christian future. Alas, the rededication often doesn't last until the evangelist leaves town. What is wrong? You simply can't *re*dedicate something that has never been dedicated.

Christian dedication is this one-time acknowledgement of the complete change of ownership, the yielding of our bodies to God. If this transaction has never been made in your life, you can rededicate your rededications until your rededicator wears out, but you will never find the "spiritual tone" or virtue you seek. Of course, *after* this presentation of our bodies, public or private rededications can be most meaningful and helpful.

Dr. Walter L. Wilson, a well-known Bible teacher now with the Lord, tells of a big, heavy-set fellow who came to visit his services. Sunday night as Dr. Wilson was in the lobby greeting folks, he asked the overweight fellow if he had a Bible.

The man said, "I have one at home."

Dr. Wilson said, "When you go home, read Leviticus 3:16. I think God wrote it for you." The man did not return to the services until Thursday. When he came in, Dr. Wilson noticed a radiance on his face.

He said, "Doc, I went home and got out my Bible and read that verse."

The verse says, "All the fat is the Lord's," and he had about three hundred pounds of it! He said, "When I read that verse, I got down on my knees and said, 'Lord Jesus, if the fat is Yours, You may as well have the whole works. I'll give You all of it.'" And that fellow became a mightily used man of God.

It is evident that Leviticus 3:16 has a more profound meaning, but if it gets people to present their whole bodies as living sacrifices, let's apply it this way. The virtue which results is necessary in God's plan of revival.

Remember, you do not *possess* spiritual tone, nor can

you manufacture it. It is available only through the Christ who dwells within. It will be yours when you claim it from Him by presenting your body—totally and irrevocably—as a living sacrifice. It is the first character trait of the growing Christian life.

THE SECOND TRAIT: KNOWLEDGE

Knowledge, our second Christlike quality, refers to a practical understanding of spiritual principles, or insight into the Scriptures. It involves applying Bible information to specific life situations.

Of course, this knowledge does not refer to the kind gained in classrooms or seminaries. It is available only in the Lord Jesus Christ "in whom are hid all the treasures of wisdom and knowledge" (Colossians 2:3). Such knowledge is revealed only in the Scriptures, and therefore personal study of the Bible is imperative if we are to experience real personal renewal.

Bible study should not be boring. The Bible is the only way we can learn of God and His ways. We see His handiwork in nature, but if we want to know Him personally and get more intimately acquainted with Him, we must study His Word. The person who finds the Bible dull and boring needs to fall in love with the Author.

An older engaged couple were talking together one evening. The girl said, "Honey, I remember reading an old dry book years ago, and the author's name was the same as yours. It was so boring I never even finished it."

Her fiance said sheepishly, "Darling, I hate to tell you this, but I wrote that book."

Thoroughly embarrassed, she began hunting in the attic for the book, blew the dust off it, and read it again. But this time it was different. The book was so intriguing she just couldn't put it down. Every page grew more interesting than the last, and she finished the book with great enthusiasm.

Now, the book hadn't changed. What was so different? Obviously she had fallen in love with the author. This is exactly what makes the Bible the most exciting Book ever written! It is the Lord Jesus Christ in written form! In a sense you don't read or study *it*; you read and study *Him!* Any revival efforts apart from intensive Bible study will be only sham.

The Bible is the only one hundred percent trustworthy thing in the world today. Even the best people can fail you, but God's Word is sure and steadfast. In its original form, it is without error or contradiction. It is our infallible guide to success and victory in this life and contains the only map to eternal life. It is the only visible thing in the world today that is eternal. "Heaven and earth [in their present form] shall pass away, but my words shall not pass away" (Matthew 24:35). You may be sure that a closed Bible will bring spiritual defeat, no matter how many "revival meetings" you attend.

Clarence W. Hall, a former war correspondent, tells what a single copy of the Bible did for the obscure little community of Shimmabuke on the island of Okinawa. In 1913, an American missionary on his way to Japan stopped in that tiny village just long enough to make two converts, Shosei and Mojon Kina. He left a Bible with them, then moved on.

These brothers had no contact with any other Christian person or group, but in the Bible they found not only an inspiring Person on whom to pattern a life, but sound precepts on which to base a society. They passed on their Good News until every man, woman, and child in Shimmabuke became a Christian. Under the impact of the Bible, pagan customs fell away, and a Christian community was formed.

After thirty years, the American army stormed the

island. When they entered Shimmabuke, the Kinas met them and welcomed them as fellow Christians. Because the missionary had come from America, they were overjoyed to meet more American "Christians."

The GI's were flabbergasted. They toured the village and were astounded at what they saw—spotlessly clean homes and streets, a high level of health and happiness, intelligence and prosperity. They had seen many villages of unbelievable poverty, ignorance and filth, but Shimmabuke was different!

The Kina brothers, observing the Americans' amazement, mistook it for disappointment. They said, "We are sorry if we seem a backward people. We have tried to follow the Bible and honor Jesus. Perhaps if you will show us how . . ."

One old sergeant said, "I can't figure it out—this kind of people coming out of only a Bible and a couple of old guys who wanted to be like Jesus! Maybe we've been using the wrong kind of weapons to make this world over."

Perhaps this is all America needs today—people who will let the Word guide them in all they do. The great evangelist, Dwight L. Moody, once said, "I have never seen a useful Christian who was not a student of God's Word."

Mr. Moody was right! Many of us have tried to substitute church activity for Bible study, but without a devotional life we are certain to live in spiritual defeat. Victory comes when we get alone with our God in His Word.

In 1945, a young man was sailing to his first term of missionary service in China. Aboard the same ship was the veteran missionary, Dr. Robert E. Speer, head of the young man's mission board. A theological discussion developed between the two men.

Dr. Speer said, "Please go to your cabin and get your Bible so we can see what the Word of God says."

The young missionary replied, "I am sorry. I packed my Bible in my trunk, and it's in the hold of the ship. I can't get it until our voyage is over."

Dr. Speer asked, "Do you mean to tell me that you are making this three-week trip without your Bible?" When the young man admitted this was the case, Dr. Speer said, "When you get to China, take the first boat home. No man is worthy to be a missionary anywhere who can keep his Bible closed for three weeks." And he sent the young man home.

We need men of Dr. Speer's caliber today! The Bible furnishes the knowledge we need to add to our faith, whether we are serving in China or in the U.S. Bible Belt. There is no alternate plan. God's Word is necessary for revival.

THE THIRD TRAIT: TEMPERANCE

Temperance is the mastery of temptations which come from within. The word literally means "holding in" of passions, appetites, and instincts so that they are our slaves and not our masters. This is often referred to as *self-control,* but self-control is dangerous unless it comes from submission to the indwelling Holy Spirit. It would be better termed *Spirit-control,* for Peter emphasized that every passion and desire should be under the perfect control and mastery of the Holy Spirit.

Most sin problems are of our own making. Though we are quick to blame others, or to say, "The devil made me do it," our real problem is self. The Lord Jesus said, "For out of the heart proceed evil thoughts, murders, adulteries, fornications, thefts, false witness, blasphemies: These are the things which defile a man" (Matthew 15:19, 20a).

Defilement comes from within. Temperance is the mastery of these things. We do not possess this mastery.

Victory comes only through the Lord Jesus, who dwells within. He *is* our temperance.

In this area, swapping out works well. When we live as we want to in the flesh, our defilement is evident. In our carnality we can only testify as did Paul, "O wretched man that I am! who shall deliver me from the body of this death?" (Romans 7:24). Paul learned that deliverance came through swapping out, letting the indwelling Christ live his life. ". . . Not I, but Christ liveth in me: and the life which I now live in the flesh I live by the faith of the Son of God, who loved me, and gave himself for me" (Galatians 2:20).

Consider a few of the swaps we can make: Instead of living in worry (a sin which says, "Christ is inadequate to meet my needs"), fear, or an attitude of perpetual griping, we can swap for His peace. "Peace I leave with you, my peace I give unto you: not as the world giveth, give I unto you. Let not your heart be troubled, neither let it be afraid" (John 14:27). Victory over these degrading sins comes by "casting all your care upon him; for he careth for you" (I Peter 5:7).

A few years ago I came to the assumption that, no matter how long I lived, I would die an extreme worrier, suffering deep fits of depression, with an uncontrollable temper. Somehow the fact that the Lord Jesus could give victory over these sins of disposition escaped me. After all, I was a "natural-born worrier," and my temper must have been inherited, and it's not hard to be depressed when world conditions are so bad. I concluded that I'd just have to live with these traits as constant plagues in my life. There just wasn't anything to do about them.

However, this is not true. The same Lord who gives people victory over adultery, drug addiction, drunkenness, lying, and cheating is equally concerned about giving victory over dispositions. It is totally unchristian to worry. No Christian has the right to lose his or her temper. Depression is a tool of the devil, and the companion sins of griping, self-pity, jealousy, and grouchiness are all anti-God. It is likely that more Christians lose spiritual victory in these matters than in the more flagrant sins of the flesh.

Victory in these areas is possible through swapping out. At first, since I was a champion worrier, I found myself giving this sin over to God hundreds of times each day. I had practiced the sin for so long that it was difficult to give my problems over to the Lord and leave them with Him.

"Lord, You just got another problem" became the watchword of my life as I attempted to claim His peace from Philippians 4:6-7. Then, this phrase was soon followed by, "Lord, I'm sorry. I'm worrying about it again." And again! And again! And soon the Lord understood what I meant when I said, "Ditto!"

But as days and weeks passed, there were fewer "agains" and "dittos." As I continued to swap out these worries, I progressively gained God's peace. Added victory began to come over those sins of self-pity, griping, and depression. While today I cannot testify to complete victory (I'm a slow learner!), I can state emphatically that God does trade His peace for all these life-wreckers if we want to swap them. I find the indwelling Lord Jesus an adequate solution for small problems—and big ones, too.

For example, I had worried severely throughout my entire life about the death of my parents. The very thought of their passing away was a phobia. I had just begun learning the secret of swapping out when news of my dad's death came. It hit me hard. I hate death! I was on the other side of the world and couldn't even get home for the funeral. This was too big a problem for me. Suddenly I realized that the Victor over death and the grave dwelled in me. I turned the whole problem over to Him. Though I was grief-stricken, the Lord gave me one of the greatest weeks of spiritual joy I've ever experienced.

Bad temper can also be swapped out. For this I had to learn a new prayer: "Take it quick, Lord." It doesn't sound too dignified, but it works because the world's greatest Temper-Keeper lives in the world's greatest temper-loser. I have never liked losing my temper. I have always regretted it afterward. I had tried so hard for years to control it. But progressive victory began only when I turned my temper over to Him in exchange for His calm.

One day I went to the Taiwan traffic bureau to register a change of address. The lines were long, the Chinese were continually shoving in front of me, and I was growing more angry by the minute as I was sent from one window to another. I reached my boiling point when a Chinese clerk refused to return my car registration until I paid a car tax of more than one hundred dollars which was not due for another month.

I went to our mission treasurer, got the money, returned to stand in more lines, and finally paid the tax. Four hours after I entered the building, I got to the last window. When that clerk asked for one hundred dollars NT (about $2.25) for making the address change, I exploded. And it didn't help to discover that I was out of Chinese money!

Loudly I told everyone in that crowded building what I thought of their traffic bureau, their lines, their inefficiency, and their whole country! And I was a Christian missionary! Let me assure any of you who helped pay my missionary salary that day that you wasted the Lord's money. Even though I returned to apologize, my temper had done its damage.

About six weeks later, I learned that I had to go back to the same bureau—this time to change my car registration. I panicked. If it took four hours just to make an address change, this would be an all-day job. But I was slowly learning how to swap-out, and I was finding the Lord Jesus extremely practical. I decided that registering the car would have to be His business.

As I left home early on the appointed morning, my wife reminded me to keep my temper, but I assured her that it had been turned over to my Temper-Keeper.

Same traffic bureau, same long lines, same shoving, same inefficiency, but this time the situation was entirely different. The same Lord who could see me through a death problem was now seeing me through an insignificant matter that would have been too much for me. It's such routine and trivial matters that often rob us of spiritual victory.

With Him in control, I did not even have to struggle with my temper. I took shoving and pushing in stride because He is used to being shoved around, all the way to the cross. I didn't have to fake a thing. Those who contributed to my salary that day made a good missionary investment. The Chinese could see Christ living in me, which is what Christianity is all about. What a difference it makes when He is on the throne of our lives!

As a finale, an old Chinese gentleman insisted on fastening my new license plates to my car, and he would accept no pay. I drove away sensing greater revival victory from changing my car registration than I receive in most church meetings. I need a God who can handle the mundane things of life for me.

Swapping out works! Instead of being frustrated by our inadequacy and inability to accomplish anything, we can swap for the power of the Holy Spirit. This is exactly what Paul did, for he testified, "I can do all things through Christ, [who pours the power into me]" (Philippians 4:13a, literal translation). It works!

Instead of succumbing to hatred, we can swap for Christ's love. Human love isn't strong enough to allow us to love our enemies. That takes divine love! "The love of God is shed abroad in our hearts by the Holy Ghost [Spirit]" (Romans 5:5b). The way to victory is in swapping out our hatred for His love. It works!

Instead of being overcome with impurity, lust, adultery, lying, or stealing, we can swap out these sins for His victory. Christians do not win victory over sins; we receive the victory as a gift from God. "But thanks be to God, which giveth us the victory through our Lord Jesus Christ" (I Corinthians 15:57). *We are not commanded to fight sin. The battle is the Lord's! We gain the victory by submitting to Him.*

A little girl learned how to apply this Biblical principle. Questioned by the deacons for church membership, she said, "I used to hear the devil knocking, and when I tried to chase him away, he'd force the door open and overwhelm me. Then I realized that the Lord Jesus lived in me. When the devil knocks now, I send Jesus to answer the door. Every time the devil sees Jesus standing there, he says 'Oops! Wrong door,' and he flees."

There is no sin or problem in life that is too big or too small for Jesus Christ. We can swap out everything that we are and cannot do for everything that He is and can do. All the resources of Heaven are ours for the asking.

THE FOURTH TRAIT: PATIENCE

Patience is the mastery of problems which come from without. It involves yielding to God without complaint—in spite of our circumstances. It is a steadfastness which allows us to stay under the load, anticipating victory through strong knowledge that "all things work together for good to them that love God, to them who are the called according to his purpose [which is to conform us to the image of his Son]" (Romans 8:28). Patience is brave, courageous acceptance of everything that life can bring to us.

Patience is not a natural quality. Some who claim to be

patient are merely lazy or suffering from low thyroid. Real steadfastness and endurance is found only in the Lord Jesus as we swap out our impatience.

During the most crucial days of the war, our American crews had to fly dangerous missions into Vietnam. An unusual number of our men were being killed. The stress on our church families was cruel, for we never knew who might be in services for the last time.

Joe attended Wednesday prayer meeting the night before he was to fly such a mission. That evening we studied the comforting truth of God's leadership in a Christian's life: "The steps of a good man are directed and established of the Lord, and He [the Lord] busies Himself with his [the good man's] every step" (Psalm 37:23, Amplified).

When Joe returned two weeks later, he told about flying low over enemy lines to drop supplies to our troops. Tracer bullets were visible everywhere, and enemy fire was hitting the plane frequently. Joe decided right then to swap out his intense fear for Christ's peace. Over and over the thought came to him, *the steps of a good man are ordered by the Lord, and He busies Himself with every step.* Joe decided that the Lord would take care of him even in such ugly, helpless circumstances. His testimony was beautiful: "Swapping out works—even when you're being shot at in an airplane over Vietnam."

Our Christian duty is not to try to change our circumstances. We were never promised easy times in this world. In fact, the Lord Jesus promised that "in the world ye shall have tribulation." The advantage for the Christian is found in the conclusion of the verse, "but be of good cheer; I have overcome the world" (John 16:33). The Overcomer lives in us, and in Him, patience is developed. Christianity is never a do-it-yourself religion.

Instead of depression and self-pity, every Christian, regardless of circumstances, should be living in joy.

"These things have I spoken unto you, that my joy might remain in you, and that your joy might be full" (John 15:11). Joy does not mean running around like a grinning idiot, faking happiness, or shouting, "Praise the Lord" after every sentence. (Some Christians seem to have a case of "holy hiccups.")

Joy is a fruit of the Spirit that brings calm assurance and victory in every circumstance. We cannot rejoice in every circumstance, but we can rejoice in the Lord in that circumstance. We can swap out our misery for the joy of the Lord. It works!

H. G. Spafford, a Christian businessman, suffered serious financial reverses and the loss of his home in the great Chicago fire. While making readjustments, he sent his wife and four daughters to live with friends in France. In mid-ocean, the French steamer collided with another ship and sank in twelve minutes, with 230 people losing their lives.

Spafford's four daughters were drowned, but Mrs. Spafford was rescued. Overcome with sadness, Spafford set sail to join his wife in Europe. Grief overwhelmed him as the ship's captain pointed out the spot of the tragedy. In that darkest of moments Spafford realized that Heaven's resources were available, that the indwelling Christ was adequate for even those tragic circumstances.

Putting all his trust in the Lord, he wrote one of the greatest of all Christian hymns:

> *When peace, like a river, attendeth my way,*
> *When sorrows like sea billows roll!*
> *Whatever my lot, Thou hast taught me to say,*
> *It is well, it is well with my soul.*

What an example of swapping out! Mr. Spafford knew how to cope with life's biggest problems by turning them over to the Lord. The third verse of "It Is Well With My

Soul" shows that he also knew the way of salvation by swapping out his sin for God's Son. It is one of the clearest explanations of salvation to be found in any hymnal:

> *My sin, O the bliss of this glorious thought,*
> *My sin, not in part, but the whole*
> *Is nailed to the cross, and I bear it no more,*
> *Praise the Lord, praise the Lord, O my soul.*

Knowing that God had been able to take care of his biggest problem (sin) at the cross, Mr. Spafford was able to swap out the daily issues of life and live in victory, even during one of the darkest crises that could come to a man.

Swapping out works not only in the big issues of life or death of loved ones, terminal illnesses, family breakups, and other such serious matters; it is equally effective in relieving the smallest pressures.

A missionary friend in Taiwan discovered that his passbook containing keys and important cards had been stolen from his car. As he proceeded toward the police station, he realized that notifying the Chinese police would be a time-consuming and futile activity. Ridiculous as it may seem to the carnal mind, he decided instead to notify the Lord and to ask Him to get the stolen goods returned.

A few days later, a wealthy Chinese gentleman drove up to the gates of the seminary where the missionary taught and returned the passbook to the gateman. When contacted, he explained that he had seen the passbook for sale on a downtown side street. Realizing it was stolen property, he bought it for the equivalent of 12½¢ American money so that he could return it to its owner. God works in mysterious ways, His wonders to perform! How many worrisome headaches could be avoided if we learned to cast both our big and our small cares upon Him!

The forces of evil are exceedingly strong, and they are

all about us. Other people are not really our problem, though they often appear to be. Paul points out that we ". . . wrestle not against flesh and blood, but against principalities, against powers, against the rulers of the darkness of this world, against spiritual wickedness in high places" (Ephesians 6:12).

No Christian is a match for these forces of evil from the supernatural realm. Satan and his demon hosts are too much for any of us. The battle is the Lord's! "Ye are of God, little children, and have overcome them: because greater is he that is in you, than he that is in the world" (I John 4:4). Our victory over circumstances—*patience*—comes through complete reliance on the Christ who dwells within.

Our lives are designed by God to produce the character of Jesus Christ in us. We all experience pressures and periods of darkness. The patient Christian will recognize that the trying events of life are simply His hand working in us, shaping us to be the kind of people He wants.

THE FIFTH TRAIT: GODLINESS

Godliness involves acting and reacting as Christ would in every circumstance. Perhaps reactions are harder to control than actions, usually because there is no time to plan a reaction. Only when the Lord Jesus is in control can we respond in the spirit of grace and holiness.

Godliness just doesn't come natural to us. No human being likes to turn the other cheek. Every bone, muscle, and fiber in me cries out, "I'll get even with you if it's the last thing I do." But the Christ who dwells within never tried getting revenge. Only He can produce a gracious reaction in me.

In similar fashion, I hate going the second mile. But if Christ is operating in me, I'll not insist on my rights. He never did! When Christ lives in me, I will serve others without counting the cost.

The outside world has a right to see godly actions in Christians. The Bible teaches this as the prime method of witnessing. "But sanctify the Lord God in your hearts: and be ready always to give an answer to every man that asketh you a reason of the hope that is in you with meekness and fear" (I Peter 3:15).

Not many lost people seem to be asking Christians these days about that hope. Often they do not see the godliness we are supposed to exhibit. They do not see Christ living out His life in us.

As a result, we resort to the pressure tactics, gimmicks, and entertainment which characterize our "revivals." Instead of answering the questions of the lost, we cram the plan of salvation down their throats. Godly living by Christians is the best antidote to these false methods, for when lost people see what Christ can do in a life, they do ask about the way of victory. We need Demonstration Evangelism!

A friend of mine is a deacon in a church that places heavy emphasis on a bold approach in telling people about salvation. Like many other good Christians, this method does not suit his personality. His "soul-winning weakness" has been a source of real frustration to him.

Late one Saturday afternoon he went for a haircut, not realizing that he had arrived inside the shop just at closing time. The barber, living close to the church, had been the target of many persuasive soul winners. He had heard all the gospel presentations devised by man, yet he showed no interest in becoming a Christian.

When my friend noticed the shop had been cleaned, he inquired about the closing time. The barber said, "Yes, I was closing, but you beat me to it. Once inside, you're entitled to your haircut."

The deacon immediately got out of the chair and said,

"No way, I'm not going to make you work overtime. I'll be back Tuesday morning."

The next day the barber attended services, and became a Christian a short time later. While we cannot minimize the work of the extrovertish soul-winners, the barber testified that the Christian kindness shown by the deacon in relinquishing his rights was his real introduction to Jesus.

It would be interesting to know how many unbelievers are waiting to see Christ living in us. The plan of salvation is just so many words if it is not accompanied by a Christ-like life. Many energetic soul-winning techniques are too harsh, stereotyped, and loveless. Real Christian kindness is a trait for which we can swap out. When Christians show that the Lord Jesus makes a difference in their lives, they earn the right to tell about Him.

Christians who are living as they please would help more if they would keep quiet! For example, godliness involves honesty, and honesty involves paying bills on time. The Christian who goes around soul-winning with a lot of past-due bills would honor God more if he spent that time arranging an honest settlement of his debts with his creditors. It is hypocrisy to witness to the lost if the indwelling Christ hasn't even made a person honest.

The same is true in home and job situations. The man who turns his wife and children away from the Lord because of his ungodly traits—temper, worry, lack of spiritual leadership, dishonesty, adultery—isn't being a faithful Christian when he tries to win strangers. The man who alienates his boss and fellow workers with his slothfulness hardly qualifies for church visitation. Young people who cheat their way through school have great difficulty convincing their friends that "Christ makes a difference."

Lost friends have very practical problems. They are looking for a faith that works. We can be certain they will ask questions about our faith *if* they see that Jesus Christ makes a practical difference in our lives seven days a week, fifty-two weeks a year. We will have many opportunities to share our faith if we have experienced His victory over sin, fear, and worry. Our next-door neighbors will be interested if they see a home abounding in love and peace.

In these unsettling times, people want more than a ticket to Heaven. The world is saying, "Sure, Christ can take me to Heaven someday, but can He do anything for me in this sin-cursed world before I get there?" The godliness we exhibit in a Christ-filled life furnishes the answer and gives us opportunity to tell what the Lord Jesus has done for us.

Godliness plays a vital role in God's plan for spiritual rejuvenation! A godly pastor's enemies hired a detective to "get the goods on him" so they could fire him. (Not too godly a group!) Thirteen weeks after the surveillance began, the detective came to the pastor and said, "After watching your life, I am sick of my sin. I want to know your God."

The detective, realizing that this confession might cause him to lose his license and his job, received the Lord Jesus as his Saviour. Godliness in the lives of believers will always make an impact on the lost.

THE SIXTH TRAIT: BROTHERLY LOVE

Brotherly love is genuine affection and concern for Christian brothers. It involves a willingness to bear the burdens of others, with a desire to move in and help. It promotes "body life" in a church.

While traveling about our country in Bible conference work, I have visited many strife-torn churches. Fellowships were split over such issues as a pastor's use of an overhead projector in teaching God's Word.

In one town, a distraught Christian spent a friendless night in desperation, finally taking her own life, while her church argued through a three-hour business meeting about debronzing an ornamental cross.

Real problems go unsolved, and great spiritual victories go unclaimed, while we argue over matters that don't make two cents' worth of difference. Certainly, "revival meetings" are not the answer for such churches. The harmony and kindness which the indwelling Christ promotes is the only solution.

Have you noticed the Jekyll and Hyde members in some churches? Charming, loving people turn into vicious, hateful ogres in business meetings. Brotherly kindness is completely ignored. The most deadly member of a church is that person who never shows any concern for spiritual matters, yet plays a leading role in church business matters—often exhibiting a spirit quite unlike that displayed by Christ.

Of course, the need for brotherly kindness is not confined to church business meetings. Everywhere in this world people are in desperate need of kind words, kind deeds, and kind friends. The Lord Jesus is always kind, and when He lives in us, we can meet the needs of others.

Is there someone you don't like, or someone who has hurt your feelings, or someone you can't forgive? Better turn these problems over to the Lord immediately. They can wreck your entire testimony.

In warning believers not to grieve the Holy Spirit, Paul wrote, "Be ye kind one to another, tenderhearted, forgiving one another, even as God for Christ's sake hath forgiven you" (Ephesians 4:32).

Kindness is one of the chief traits in a truly revived person or a truly revived church.

THE SEVENTH TRAIT: LOVE

Love is looking at people from God's viewpoint. This *agape* love is the same kind of love God has for the unjust, the rebellious, the guilty sinner. It is extended toward those who are unlovely. It is a sacrificial love which seeks to promote the highest good in others.

This is not natural love. It is not sentimentality. It is not based on emotions. It is a love which only Christians can possess because it is "... shed abroad in our hearts by the Holy Ghost [Spirit] . . ." (Romans 5:5). When the Bible says, "God is love" (I John 4:8), it refers to this kind of love. Only when the Lord lives in us can we experience this highest form of love.

The Greek language has a number of different words which could be translated "love." *Eros* is a lustful love—I love you for what I can get from you. *Phileo* is conditional love, a love of equals—I love you *because* you love me. But *agape* is "in spite of" love, a love that stoops, sacrifices, and forgives—I love you *in spite of* what you are, *in spite of* what you do. *Agape* depends on the lover (the indwelling Christ) rather than on the "lovee."

Agape love is the heart of Christianity. This love of the unlovely sent the Lord Jesus to Calvary to die for sinners—for you, and for me. The Lord told us that this love is the evidence to the world that our Christianity is genuine. "By this shall all men know that ye are my disciples, if ye have love one to another" (John 13:35). *Agape* is the identifying mark of all true believers.

The truly distinguishing trait of *agape* is that it is love for enemies. The Lord Jesus, in commanding us to love our enemies, goes on to state that anyone can love his friends. It doesn't take any Christianity for you to love those who love you (Matthew 5:46,47), but Christianity is based on this highest of concepts—love of enemies.

Not a single human being possesses this kind of love.

Some try hard to imitate it or counterfeit it, but in reality it is only when Christ dwells in our hearts that we are rooted and grounded in *agape* (Ephesians 3:17). *Agape* can never be manufactured by us.

In the Lord's intercessory prayer on the eve of the cross, He said, "O righteous Father ... I have declared unto them thy name, and will declare it: that the love wherewith thou hast loved me may be in them, and I in them" (John 17:25a, 26).

On that same night He spoke to His disciples, "As the Father hath loved me, so have I loved you: continue ye in my love" (John 15:9). Again, the secret lies in swapping out our hatred for His love. We allow Him to love our enemies through us. And it works!

At the lowest point in my Christian life that first year in Taiwan, I discovered that I had made a rather large number of enemies. I was grieved when I read about hatred and love in God's Word:

"He that saith he is in the light, and hateth his brother, is in darkness even until now" (I John 2:9).

"We know that we have passed from death unto life, because we love the brethren. He that loveth not his brother abideth in death" (I John 3:14).

"If a man say, I love God, and hateth his brother, he is a liar: for he that loveth not his brother whom he hath seen, how can he love God whom he hath not seen? And this commandment have we from him, That he who loveth God love his brother also" (I John 4:20, 21).

It is so clear! I cannot be right with God if I am not right with others. In fact, I can't really worship God or give gifts to Him until I attempt to mend my relationships with others (Matthew 5:23, 24).

If I am unwilling to forgive others (strangely enough, it has always been the other guy's fault!), I cannot receive forgiveness (Matthew 6:14, 15).

Then, too, hatred makes me a poor witness because love

of enemies is my badge of discipleship (John 13:34, 35). What a dilemma for one who hates!

Since I personally had to do something about this, I did the pious thing. I began praying that God would change all those people I hated! Wasn't that gracious of me? I was like the fellow who got limburger cheese in his moustache and went about saying, "This room stinks, and this room stinks." Then he opened the door, looked outside and said, "The whole world stinks."

What a hard lesson I had to learn! When a Christian hates someone, the problem is not that someone. We need to check our own moustaches! Without any doubt, the problem is me.

Hating someone is perhaps the greatest evidence that Jesus Christ is not on the throne in my life. When He is in control, I will love even my enemies.

Through His strength and love, I went to some people, called others, and wrote to still others to straighten out messes I had made. I even paid back money I had stolen twenty-seven years before. In every instance, my new friends granted me forgiveness. In several cases, doors of opportunity were opened to share my faith. One lady said, "I haven't been right with the Lord for twelve years, but I believe I can get right tonight." This is what personal revival is all about.

Please note that I am not really the confessing type. It isn't natural for me. I hate to say, "I'm sorry." I want to rationalize that "it was their fault, not mine," but the Lord Jesus will not allow His people to continue with a host of enemies. No matter how hard you try to live abundantly or to promote revival in your church, you will be a barrier to blessing, a hindrance to renewal, if you bear hatred or bitterness toward anyone, or leave any sin unconfessed in your life.

Although I can't possibly love my enemies, the Lord Jesus can love them for me and through me. Several of my closest friends today were once bitter enemies. What a great Christ we have!

Earl and Lois Langley are two of the most effective missionaries I've seen in action. Sent to Taiwan to serve as dorm parents in a missionary school, their hearts were drawn to the spiritual needs of young Chinese university students, although the Chinese were not their missionary assignment. Earl was a retired businessman, not a preacher, and his Chinese language study was only slightly worse than mine! Undoubtedly we were the two poorest students in the history of the Chinese language institute; yet, the Langleys consistently led Chinese young people to faith in Christ. Their trophies of grace exist throughout the island and in several American universities.

How did they do it? Real Christian love. The Langleys' love of the Chinese caused them to open their living room each evening to scores of students for English classes, and the Bible served as the textbook. Dozens of Chinese young people are now Christians because the Langleys cared enough to open their hearts—and their living room—day after day, night after night.

It cost them their privacy. Sometimes students took advantage of their hospitality. It wasn't always easy. However, few missionaries have experienced the response the Langleys received. God's love for the Chinese shines so brightly through their lives that they no longer serve as dorm parents but spend all their time ministering to their Chinese friends.

I cannot forget a statement Earl Langley made to me as we first sailed to Taiwan. "I don't know why I'm going to Taiwan," he said. "Although I'll be working primarily with Americans, I'll be living in a Chinese world. I have never been around Asians before, and I have no special love for them." Then he added, "But I know God can give me love for them."

The evidence points to the fact that God can give us love for any individual or group of people. The Chinese have seen the love of God in the Langleys' hearts. It is a love that overshadows all obstacles and makes the Christian life effective and purposeful. It is a love that makes serving Christ a joyous experience.

How is your love life? Are there visits that need to be made or letters that need to be written? Do you need to return stolen goods or make something right? Are you prejudiced toward other races? If you have a hate life, you will be on the spiritual shelf until you let the indwelling Christ make it right. There will be not a trace of spiritual rejuvenation in your life, no matter how hard you work toward it.

A word of caution about confession and forgiveness: Confession should be only as public as the sin. If you hate someone, or have a grievance with him—and he knows it—go to him. However, if he does not know of your hatred, confess it only to God. Great harm is done in so-called "confessional meetings" when Christians surprise others with confessions of hatred and dislike, when the second party was unaware that a problem existed. Deep hurt and distrust often result from such unbiblical practices.

These seven marks of progress are the key to victorious Christian living and to God's kind of revival. Griffith-Thomas points out that "faith is the foundation and love the culmination, and every grace in between springs out of faith and is intended to be expressed ultimately in love."

These graces cover all our relationships and attitudes. We cannot be satisfied with accomplishing them one at a time. They are all available in the Lord Jesus Christ, for God has "... given unto us all things that pertain unto life and godliness..." (II Peter 1:3). Spiritual renewal, just like salvation, is a gift from God.

4
Living
The Abundant Life

*T*he burning desire of every Christian should be to become a fruitful Christian; the alternative is to remain useless and unproductive. But how can we become fruitful Christians?

> *For if these things be in you, and abound, they make you that ye shall neither be barren nor unfruitful in the knowledge of our Lord Jesus Christ (1:8).*

"These things" are in us if we have received the Lord Jesus as Saviour, for then we become partakers of the divine nature (1:4). But they are not a spasmodic possession, present one time and absent the next. All "these things" are readily available as we appropriate the resources of Christ. Each person who has given his life to Christ possesses all seven marks of spiritual progress.

However, the key to spiritual rejuvenation is in the word *abound*. It refers to the Spirit-filled life which always overflows into the lives of others. When we allow the Spirit of Christ to control our lives, others will be spiritually refreshed. Our virtue, knowledge, temperance, patience, godliness, brotherly kindness, and love will always bring spiritual success to others. We will not be barren, idle, or ineffective if these traits of Christ are overflowing in our lives.

Our Christian fulfillment does not depend primarily on

what we do but upon what we are. Character comes before conduct; belief comes before behavior. Often our churches emphasize doing things rather than being something for God. Service is not the door to Jesus; Jesus is the door to service. Many people "superabound" in church work; yet their lives are barren and unfruitful. God's guarantee in this verse is that if we exhibit Christ-like character we will not be useless and ineffective.

Many hard-working church people need to remember that Jesus said, "I am the vine, ye are the branches: He that abideth in me, and I in him, the same bringeth forth much fruit; for without me ye can do nothing" (John 15:5). We are the branches, and branches never produce fruit; they bear it.

Our revival programs often do not operate under this principle. We frustrate people to the point of despair by trying to get them to work to produce victory. All the life-giving sap is in the vine; it merely flows through the branches, and when it does, we bear fruit.

Have you ever seen branches on a fruit tree twisting, sweating, struggling, squeezing, in an effort to produce fruit? It doesn't happen in nature, but it is often noticeable in branches that go by such names as Baptists, Methodists, Pentecostals, and the like.

The most important spiritual lesson many of us need to learn is to relax in the Lord and let Him produce the fruit. True spiritual victory comes from *being,* not *doing.* Of course, this does not mean that a Christian will be lazy. The person filled with the character of Christ will not be idle but will be accomplishing God's work in God's way, not running himself ragged in useless committee work or unnecessary church programs.

THE EFFECT OF CHRIST-CONTROLLED LIVING

Randy, an Air Force pilot, confessed his barrenness and

unfruitfulness in sharing Christ with others, although he had been a faithful participant in church activities for many years. After he was shown the importance of personal devotions and daily Bible study, he developed into a faithful student of the Word. In just a few weeks, he led Jim another pilot, to faith in Christ. Both men then became zealous students of God's Word.

Within a few months, Jim presented himself at the close of a service to inform the church that God had called him to preach. At the same time, a young pilot and his wife asked to unite with our fellowship. However, Don, a Baptist preacher's son, was hesitant when asked if he had been born again.

I planned to talk with him after the service about his lack of assurance, but he and his wife were eager to talk with Jim, and the three of them left together. That evening Don came back to publicly acknowledge that he had just invited Jesus Christ into his life as a result of Jim's witness, explaining that "everything my dad taught me moved from my head to my heart this afternoon."

Don and Jim then told this story. Two years before, these young pilots had made a flight together. In a motel room, they had begun talking about God. Jim, a confirmed Lutheran, and Don, raised in a Baptist parsonage, both agreed that God was not real and that the Christian faith was a farce.

Today, two years later, they had met in the front of a Baptist church in Taichung, Taiwan. Don's religious opinions had not changed, but Jim was different, and the difference showed on his face. Noticing this change, Don requested an explanation. When Jim told how God had given him new life, Don, too, dedicated his life to Christ.

Don's salvation and assurance became especially comforting a few months later when we learned that his plane had been shot down in Vietnam. Don had given his life for his country, but he lives on, "absent from the body, but present with the Lord." His faith shone brightly in the two notes written to his wife shortly before leaving on his final flight. But Don's testimony did not end with those notes. Like Abel, we can say of Don, "He being dead, yet speaketh."

Dr. Jess Moody conducted a televised memorial service for Don at the First Baptist Church in West Palm Beach, Florida. The Air Force sent four Thunderbird jets to fly overhead in the "Missing Man" formation. Just as the formation passed over the cross atop the church building, one plane peeled off from the group, pointed toward the sky and shot straight up like a rocket, piercing the clouds and vanishing into a cloud bank.

The face of Don's mother lit up. She clapped her hands, her face streaked with tears, and shouted, "That is just what happened to Don. He went straight to Heaven. Oh, it's so wonderful! It's wonderful!"

In a West Palm Beach motel room, a distressed young man watched this service and wrote a letter to Dr. Moody. He told of illness which had crippled him, of domestic problems which had caused his wife to leave him, and of discouragement which caused him to contemplate suicide. He then related the effects of the memorial service and Dr. Moody's sermon on his life. Limping into his bedroom, he had knelt down to pray. As he received the Lord Jesus into his life, a wonderful sense of peace he had never known before came over him.

As the Lord moved into his heart he was able to throw away his cane and return to work. Reconciliation with his wife soon followed. The blessings of the Lord continued to grow sweeter and richer in his life as he began serving in his church. Spiritual victory shone through his letter as he thanked Dr. Moody for leading him to Christ.

And so the fruit-bearing from these lives goes on and on. Randy continues to be used of the Lord to reach people wherever he is stationed. His Christian influence is no longer barren. Jim has just been graduated from seminary and approved for foreign mission service, and the television viewer has found a new, wonderful life worth living. This is God's fruit, the kind that remains! It is what He wants every Christian to experience.

THE EFFECT OF SELF-CONTROLLED LIVING

In contrast to the healthy, fruitful Christian of verse 8, we now see in verse 9 the saddest sight—the carnal Christian, a person who has been genuinely born again but is not letting Christ live his life. He is the most pathetic of all people, a babe in Christ who has never grown or developed by appropriating the graces listed in verses 5-7.

The carnal man has an inadequate view of salvation, having seen nothing except deliverance from everlasting fire. What a miserably defective view! This man may attend revival meetings, teach a Sunday School class, or serve as a pastor. He may try to reach others, but in reality he is a hindrance to revival because he is spiritually blind. In fact, he will be an upsetting influence in his church fellowship, causing strife and division (I Corinthians 3:1-4). Carnality is undoubtedly the biggest problem in our churches today. Much of this is due to our false revival programs. Some churches never hear anything but salvation messages and soul-winning challenges. Christians may become hyperactive and at the same time be starving for the teachings they need for effective Christian living.

God's plan of salvation is a great starting place, but there is so much more! Real revival will come as the "much more" is emphasized and developed. We must add "these things" to our lives or suffer blinding carnality.

A man who had just recently discovered the principles of abundant life summed it up this way: "I received Christ eighteen years ago. I was told that I never needed to be saved again — in fact, I couldn't be! Yet, all the preaching I have heard for these past eighteen years has been 'How to Be Saved.' It has been so frustrating!"

For the past few years this man has feasted on the truths of victorious Christian living and has developed into a joyous, fruitful believer. This is revival!

The pastor who teaches only salvation is depriving his flock. Internal strife is sure to develop because his people do not grow. Furthermore, he is ignoring his job description from Heaven to "feed the flock" and "preach the Word." He may do well in the "numbers game" by baptizing many people, but he will answer to God for not presenting every man mature in Christ Jesus (Colossians 1:28).

We will never have God's kind of revival until we emphasize remembrance of "these things," developing the spiritual life and growth of those already saved. This should be the pastor's main concern, and in my experience it is best accomplished by teaching the Word in verse-by-verse exposition. I have found this to be most effective in helping people learn to observe all things which He has commanded — the part of the Great Commission for which pastors are primarily responsible.

Please note that the carnal person *is* a Christian. The latter part of verse 9 proves this; he has been purged from his old sins. But the poor fellow lacks "these things" and is living in Christian defeat. His life is hampered by a serious vision problem.

SPIRITUAL SHORT-SIGHTEDNESS

But he that lacketh these things is blind, and

> *cannot see afar off, and hath forgotten that he*
> *was purged from his old sins (1:9).*

The carnal Christian is blind (1:9a), suffering from spiritual myopia, the same Greek word that is used by eye doctors to denote nearsightedness. His defective vision assumes three forms:

Short-sightedness in His Vision of the Past

> *. . . and hath forgotten that he was purged from*
> *his old sins (1:9b).*

This is one of the hardest-to-believe verses in all Scripture. This person has been truly born again, but lacking diligence in adding the qualities of Christ to his life, he has forgotten he was cleansed from sin.

This verse should silence all those who believe that we can lose God's salvation. This man is described as saved, but he has failed to add to his faith. He has become so shortsighted that he has forgotten the time when Christ was a reality in his soul. He is blinded to that time when his heart throbbed with great emotion as he looked by faith to the cross and had the guilt and shame of his sins taken away.

His faith in the gospel has become faint and far away, but his need is not to be saved again. That's impossible! We do not lose our salvation because of what *we* do. Christ is our salvation, and so our salvation depends upon what *He* does. This is the blessed doctrine of divine seat belts! God has promised to keep us secure.

I was not saved by my actions, and I do not keep myself saved by my actions. Paul wrote, "Being confident of this very thing, that he which hath begun a good work in you will perform it until the day of Jesus Christ" (Philippians 1:6). The only way I can lose my salvation is if Christ sins — and He certainly isn't going to!

Be assured that if keeping my salvation depended upon me, I'd have lost it long ago, and you would have done no better with yours. But it doesn't depend upon us. It depends solely upon the solid Rock of Ages, the Lord Jesus Christ. If that Rock sinks, I'm sunk, but as long as the Rock stands, I stand with Him. The old Christian stated it well, "I often tremble on the Rock, but the Rock never trembles under me!"

What an awful travesty that, in the light of such "Amazing Grace," a Heaven-born soul would stray so far from the Father that he would even forget the time he was purged from his old sins. It does happen, according to the Word of God.

This backslider is not described as a drunk, or an adulterer, or as one who has quit attending church services. The only thing we know about him is that he lacks the things which Christians are to add to their faith. Such a man might frequent the saloons, or he might be a teetotaler. He may be living a gutter life, or he may be a respected religionist who exhibits no outstanding vices. Whatever his outward characteristics, the poor man has let his love for the Saviour grow cold. He needs desperately to confess his sins so he can again enjoy close fellowship with his Lord.

Just as desperately, he needs to begin adding the radiant treasures of the previous verses. He must be brought to the place where he can say, "I am crucified with Christ: nevertheless I live; yet not I, but Christ liveth in me: and the life which I now live in the flesh I live by the faith of the Son of God, who loved me, and gave himself for me" (Galatians 2:20).

Short-sightedness in His Present Vision

Wherefore the rather, brethren, give diligence to make your calling and election sure: for if ye do these things, ye shall never fall (1:10).

This nearsighted believer cannot see the things of Heaven, although he may be quick to notice worldly matters. The light of God's Word dazzles his sin-sick soul. He has no spiritual insight into the meaning of life.

Believers have only two genuine bases of assurance— the finished work of Christ and the changeless Word of God. Since both have been ignored by the carnal Christian, his spiritual life will be characterized by doubts. It is impossible to serve God acceptably or to live victoriously if one is uncertain of his heavenly calling as a child of God.

Peter advises Christians described in verse 9 to take stock of their lives. Rather than continue their present way of life, they need to diligently cultivate the seven traits of a growing Christian. A real Christian can never lose his salvation, but if he fails to add "these things," he will go through life stumbling in misery, wretchedness, and doubt.

On the other hand, when the indwelling Holy Spirit is allowed to produce overflowing Christian graces, there will be assurance of his calling and election. He will be a *revival* Christian. Any call from God leads to glorifying the Lord Jesus. If He is being glorified in our lives, then our calling and election has been made sure.

Short-sightedness in His Future Vision

For so an entrance shall be ministered unto you abundantly into the everlasting kingdom of our Lord and Saviour Jesus Christ (1:11).

God has not left us without a plan for our future. The thought of Christ's kingdom is no dreamy, impractical thing. It is the means by which we are to free ourselves from slavery to the world.

There is great spiritual victory to be gained through a long look past our present circumstances; however, this long look of faith cannot be taken by Christians who have been slothful about developing Christ's character, for they are blind and cannot see afar off. Despair results when we only see things that are near—sin, vice, indifference, and callousness of men. But we gain courage and hope when we see God.

Perhaps the key word in this verse is *abundant,* for it describes the kind of entrance the diligent Christian will have into the eternal kingdom. If we yield ourselves in obedience to God, He will lavishly equip us for life in His kingdom. But the blinded, self-serving, carnal believer will be "saved, yet . . . as by fire" (I Corinthians 3:15). That means he will barely squeeze in.

The Christian who adds virtue, knowledge, temperance, patience, godliness, brotherly kindness, and love to his faith not only insures a fruitful life on earth, but also guarantees an abundant entrance into the kingdom and future rewards in the life to come.

Two kinds of Christians will be caught up to meet the Lord in the air when He returns for His church: the spiritual believer, who has been living the Christ-controlled life, adding the resources of Christ to his faith; and the stumbling, wretched blind one, who has lived his life as he wanted, failing to appropriate the blessings Christ wanted him to have. Both will meet the Lord; one in confidence, the other in shame. "And now, little children, abide in him; that, when he shall appear, we may have confidence, and not be ashamed before him at his coming" (I John 2:28).

PETER'S PEACE ABOUT DEATH

Peter now gives personal testimony about the two

instruments—men and the Book—which God uses in propagating the faith.

> *Wherefore I will not be negligent to put you always in remembrance of these things, though ye know them, and be established in the present truth. Yea, I think it meet [fitting], as long as I am in this tabernacle, to stir you up by putting you in remembrance; Knowing that shortly I must put off this my tabernacle, even as our Lord Jesus Christ hath shewed me (1:12-14).*

Now an old man, Peter knew death was close at hand. While he had no new truth to leave his readers, he was overwhelmed with a sense of urgency to establish in them the foundational truths he had already shared. His strong desire before his departure was to "stir up" or "revive" God's people by feeding them these truths as the Lord had commanded (John 21:16, 17).

The aged apostle faced his death in peace, even though he knew it would be violent. He simply said, "I know my tabernacle, my physical body, must be folded up shortly" (verse 14, paraphrase). Peter knew that the physical death of a Christian was not to be compared with the spiritual death of an unbeliever.

Death is always separation. Physical death is temporary separation of the soul-spirit from the body—"absent from the body . . . present with the Lord" (II Corinthians 5:8). But spiritual death—real death—is separation of body, soul, and spirit from God forever.

Why was Peter so unconcerned about this matter? How could he concentrate on writing about spiritual renewal with death so near? His calmness resulted from knowledge that the Lord Jesus had taken the sting out of sin, death, and the grave, that ". . . through death he might destroy him that had the power of death, that is, the devil;

And deliver them who through fear of death were all their lifetime subject to bondage" (Hebrews 2:14, 15).

Peter knew God's estimate of Christian death. "Precious in the sight of the Lord is the death of his saints" (Psalm 116:15). He knew that a Christian dies in hope. "The wicked is driven away in his wickedness: but the righteous hath hope in his death" (Proverbs 14:32).

He knew that Christian death brings peace. "The righteous perisheth, and no man layeth it to heart: and merciful men are taken away, none considering that the righteous is taken away from the evil to come. He shall enter into peace" (Isaiah 57:1, 2a). As a result, Peter could face death with the Christian attitude, "Yea, though I walk through the valley of the shadow of death, I will fear no evil: for thou art with me" (Psalm 23:4a).

How different the death of an unsaved man! The Lord says He has no pleasure in the death of the wicked (Ezekiel 33:11). Christ rejectors have much to fear about death because they must go through it alone. In their eternal death there is no hope. "When a wicked man dieth, his expectation shall perish: and the hope of unjust men perisheth" (Proverbs 11:7).

The unbeliever's death is horrible. "My heart is sore [very] pained within me: and the terrors of death are fallen upon me. Fearfulness and trembling are come upon me, and horror hath overwhelmed me" (Psalm 55:4, 5).

Moreover I will endeavour that ye may be able after my decease to have these things always in remembrance (1:15).

Peter was aware that his departure would not destroy grace teachings. Before his demise, he made provision for his readers to have a lasting remembrance of his victory teachings. He wanted them to call on these truths whenever they might need them. His mind was on revival, not the cemetery.

THE COMING GLORY

> *For we have not followed cunningly devised fables, when we made known unto you the power and coming of our Lord Jesus Christ, but were eyewitnesses of his majesty. For he received from God the Father honour and glory, when there came such a voice to him from the excellent glory, This is my beloved Son, in whom I am well pleased. And this voice which came from heaven we heard, when we were with him in the holy mount (1:16-18).*

Peter firmly believed that Christ was going to return to earth. He assured his readers that his teachings concerning the second coming were not imaginary. He had been given a glimpse of eternal glory when he was with Jesus on the Mount of Transfiguration. He remembered so well when he, along with James and John, was privileged to look beyond this temporal world to the beauty and light of the everlasting kingdom.

Aware of the brevity of time remaining for his ministry, the apostle sought to refute the error of those who raised questions concerning the coming glory of the Lord. False teachers had accused him of following cleverly invented myths, but Peter testified concerning his personal experience of beholding the majesty, splendor, and Heavenly glory of Christ.

On the Mount of Transfiguration he was given a preview of the magnificence of the coming King! He was an eyewitness to the glory which shone through Christ's raiment. He saw the Lord Jesus as He will appear when He returns to establish His kingdom, and he actually heard God's voice from Heaven declare that Jesus was His beloved Son.

Of course he could never forget such a spectacular experience. He had seen the glorified Lord with his own eyes and had heard God's voice from Heaven with his own ears. What an experience! But Peter realized that a Christian can't live just on experiences. There is something better, something more reliable.

THE VALIDITY OF THE BIBLE

> *We have also a more sure word of prophecy; whereunto ye do well that ye take heed, as unto a light that shineth in a dark place, until the day dawn, and the day star arise in your hearts: Knowing this first, that no prophecy of the scripture is of any private interpretation. For the prophecy came not in old time by the will of man: but holy men of God spake as they were moved by the Holy Ghost [Spirit] (1:19-21).*

Peter now presents another witness to the truth of Christ's return, one that Peter regarded as even more important than his eyewitness experience. He considered the testimony of the Old Testament prophets to be more certain and reliable for his readers than his own experience. His readers weren't able to be with Christ at the Transfiguration, but they could read the message Christ gave to His prophets.

The prophetic Word of God is more convincing than any experience of the senses. The Bible is a sounder basis for faith than any signs, miracles, or experiences. Verses are more reliable than visions or voices!

We would do well to pay greater attention to the Word of God. It is extremely dangerous to base salvation or any other Christian experience on miraculous emotional happenings, events which excite the senses. Many people think they are saved or filled with the Spirit because of some tummy-warming experience, even though it be unauthorized in the Scriptures.

Any true experience which God gives is solidly based on His Word; it grows out of the Biblical message. We cannot know we are saved or Spirit-filled because of experiences we've had; our assurance must come from what God says in His Word!

The problem with relying on experiences is that the devil, too, can perform miracles. Even demons are miracle workers (Revelation 16:14). They can promote experiences which seem genuine. In a future age, the False Prophet will call down fire from the heavens and make a living statue of the Antichrist. He "deceiveth them that dwell on the earth by the means of those miracles which he had power to do" (Revelation 13:14a).

It is dangerous, therefore, for a Christian continually to seek spectacular experiences on which to base his life. Miracles are great when they grow out of God's Word. The spectacular is truly thrilling when it is Bible-based, but great caution must be exercised to ascertain that miracles are from the Lord, not from the forces of evil.

Though Peter had a magnificent experience on the Mount of Transfiguration, he stressed that such experiences are not to be the basis for our Christian faith.

The prophetic Word is a lamp shining in a dark day, giving light to the soul until that great day dawns and the Morning Star arises in our hearts. The Bible throws light on the believer's pathway until his Lord returns. This world is a dark place and it seems to be growing darker. The Bible is our only divine revelation. Apart from it, we know nothing about the meaning of life, nothing about death, and nothing about eternity. Bible study, therefore, is no luxury—is not optional. It is an absolute necessity for every person concerned about his spiritual health. It is the believer's guidebook until we see the Lord Jesus face to face.

The inspiration of the Scriptures is the basis for all Christianity. Paul wrote, "All scripture is given by inspiration of God, and is profitable for doctrine, for reproof, for correction, for instruction in righteousness: That the man of God may be perfect, throughly furnished unto all good works" (II Timothy 3:16, 17).

The Bible is of divine origin, not human. Each of the sixty-six books is God-breathed. Inspiration extends to every chapter, every sentence, every word, every "jot and tittle" in the original documents. Because the Bible is verbally inspired, it is accurate, authoritative, and reliable. No wonder Peter said we do well to heed its teachings!

The greatest tragedy of our day is that many "brilliant" Christians do not accept the verbal inspiration of the Scriptures. Jeremiah tells how Jehudi cut the sacred writings with a penknife and cast them into the fire, but this butchery is mild compared to what so-called scholarship does to the Bible today in many seminaries and pulpits.

It seems popular, a mark of intelligence, to reject all that man cannot understand, refusing to accept by faith what God has revealed. Human speculation and reasoning is substituted for divine revelation. But the Bible is one organic whole; either it is fully and completely inspired by God and is therefore wholly reliable, or it is not fully inspired and is therefore untrustworthy.

Would God give an imperfect revelation of Himself? Great revivals of the past bear witness that belief in verbal inspiration is necessary for victory, and that Bible-denying "scholarship" leads away from world-changing revival.

The Bible did not originate in the will of man. No one sat

down and decided to write a book of the Bible. The Holy Spirit guided men to write what God intended, even to the precise words He desired to use in communicating His truth. The prophet had little to do with it; he was a mere instrument. An organ is not the music; it is but the instrument through which the music is expressed. Likewise, the prophet was the instrument through which God's Word was expressed.

Since the Holy Spirit wrote the Word, He must also interpret it. That is why grandma out in the hills, filled with the Spirit, can understand spiritual truths that baffle the unregenerated genius. Paul tells us that "the natural man [unsaved] receiveth not the things of the Spirit of God: for they are foolishness unto him: neither can he know them, because they are spiritually discerned" (I Corinthians 2:14). Our attitude toward the Bible determines how much we are used in promoting or hindering revival. God has always bypassed scholarship that is busy trying to out-think Him.

Peter wanted his readers to believe God's Word, for the Word contains God's way of spiritual renewal. It is reliable because the Holy Spirit is the Originator, Designer, Producer, and Interpreter. Appropriating the Word into our lives is the only sure path to a rich, lasting, rejuvenated faith.

5
How To Spot
A Phony

Second Peter 1 tells us how God's revival blessing comes through remembering His foundational truths. Chapter 2 presents the negative side: *How Not to Do It.* Sadly enough, we often see more chapter 2 revival procedures than the God-given ones of the first chapter. No wonder there is so much heartbreak and division in churches, homes, and individual lives!

Second Peter 2 is one of the angriest chapters in the Bible. It is blistering—not from a loss of temper, but from Peter's white-hot passion. In this chapter, the aged apostle reveals the heart of God as God views false teachers leading people astray. This dark, appalling passage displays false teachers in their true light.

Believers need to study it carefully, and churches need to be alert to the dangers of these men and their counterfeit teachings. Rich blessing comes to those who profit from this exposure of the false and dare to do things God's way!

FALSE PROPHETS

> *But there were false prophets also among the people, even as there shall be false teachers among you, who privily [secretly] shall bring in damnable [destructive] heresies, even denying the Lord that bought them and bring upon themselves swift destruction (2:1).*

The introductory word *but* contrasts self-appointed religious racketeers with the holy men of God who were inspired to write Scriptures (1:21). Jesus warned that this unholy parade of "devil's disciples" which began in Old Testament times would continue until the last judgment (Matthew 7:15; Mark 13:5, 22). The apostles warned over and over that we should be on guard against the havoc that false religious leaders would cause in churches (Acts 20:29; II Timothy 4:3, 4; Titus 1:10, 11; Jude 4), and Peter devoted several paragraphs to exposing these unspiritual clergymen. Who are these false leaders?

THEIR IDENTITY

Most commentaries tend to limit II Peter 2 to cultists and outright Bible deniers. Certainly grave religious errors need to be exposed, but the warning here seems to be aimed also at more subtle heretics, those who teach enough true doctrine to become entrenched in the best of churches, then cleverly sneak in their man-made schemes and deviations from the truth.

In this chapter, Peter seems to refer to some false teachers who are eternally lost ("to whom the mist of darkness is reserved for ever," verse 17) and to others who are saved but have forsaken the right way, as was the case with Balaam (verse 15). Both the lost and the carnal believer have in common a denial of the Lord's claim on their lives. Both introduce fatal heresies to their followers. A carnal Christian can be every bit as dangerous in ministry as an unbeliever. The most important issue, therefore, is not to determine the spiritual condition of the false teachers but to realize that a corrupt clergy, saved or lost, can bring everlasting destruction to the followers whom they manipulate for their own glory.

Peter was writing a revival handbook, so necessarily

his warning would expose those who slyly attempt to destroy God's program of renewal. It would be much more comfortable for us to apply this chapter only to the cultists and to those who deny the validity of the Word of God, or to refer only to self-ambitious leaders who use church or denominational politics to climb to positions of authority. The heart of this passage, however, does not seem to be about those who substitute human speculation or personal ambition for the truth.

If the purpose of this epistle is to promote God's way of revival, as we have contended, the warning would logically be against false revivalists and their teachings. The context forces me to believe that it is primarily an expose of those who walk in evangelical circles, both pastors and evangelists, who—for the sake of money, prestige, or "visible results"—deceive people with unbiblical revival practices. They may even be saved men, but if they are, they are so carnal that they do not mind damning others for personal gain. These are real wolves in sheep's clothing. And their scriptural condemnation is shocking.

The flaming evangelist or the well-known pastor can be every bit as false and much harder to expose than the person who openly denies the inspiration of the Scriptures. His impure motives can be cloaked in a charming personality and a display of entertaining talent that mesmerizes people. It becomes unpopular to speak against this winsome fellow. He uses enough Bible to satisfy the fundamentalists, and people love his flamboyancy, not to mention his Madison Avenue wardrobe. Flesh revivalism brought about by showmanship is surely one of the biggest problems in evangelical circles today.

However, it is not the outward dress and other peculiarities that make a man false. Rather, his message, mechanics, and motivation are the serious matters which demand our careful attention. Promoting deadly flesh evangelism and revivalism which stirs only the emotions is leading many people to destruction.

Not *all* evangelists are guilty! I know several full-time evangelists who are effective, useful men of God. Their motives are pure; their message is true; and their methods are sane. These men are embarrassed by the self-promoting evangelists who advertise their own greatness, put on a religious vaudeville routine, and use unscrupulous means to get people down the aisle and to collect big offerings. True God-called evangelists suffer heartache over such antics.

And not *only* evangelists are guilty! The "numbers racket" has invaded churches to the point that many pastors involve themselves in flesh evangelism. Getting people down the aisles, by hook or by crook, is all that seems important. In fact, the sensational evangelist would be out of business if numbers-crazy pastors did not invite him to preach in their churches.

A pastor friend recently confessed that he is hosting a high-pressure evangelistic team for the third time, even though he does not appreciate their ministry, because they are "the only ones who can draw a crowd and get my people excited."

Against this type ministry Peter directed his attack. Flesh evangelism and revival circuses may excite men, but they have never been what God had in mind to bring real revival.

Peter described false teachers as those who secretly bring in heresies of destruction—false principles which seek to destroy the truth. The leaders themselves, oozing charm and talent, could actually be Christians, bought by the blood of Christ, but their chief sin is that they are rejecting the Lord's claim on their lives and ministries. They have denied Jesus the opportunity to be Lord of their lives. Facing ruin themselves, they lead others down a path which could even lead to eternal destruction.

It may be argued that these revivalists cannot be false because they "preach Jesus." But do they tell the true story of salvation and of the Christian life? Almost any man can put together a few sermons that will appeal to people's emotions, and any preacher can get people down an aisle with gimmicks, emotional appeals, tear-jerking stories, and endless invitations. However, emotional bubblebaths in front of a church have yet to save a single soul.

True salvation involves a change of man's will. The convert comes under new ownership. The New Testament message is far deeper than "receiving Jesus as Saviour" or "walking the aisle for Jesus" or "coming forward to be counted for Jesus." Biblical salvation calls for the believer to put an "Under New Management" sign on his life. Jesus Christ must become Lord. Self must abdicate the throne.

However, since few people respond quickly to this message, there is a tendency to drop the lordship theme and offer a shallow salvation that builds statistics but damns souls.

An energetic evangelist recently noted that the ten churches which led his state convention in baptisms all used full-time evangelists. This fact has no real significance, for churches and pastors operate so differently that their numerical results cannot be logically compared.

One church may be content to baptize people just to count them. This church needs only a fleet of buses, lots of bubble gum and prizes, and an overly persuasive evangelist to out-baptize all other churches.

Another church may be far less concerned with numbers because it wants statistics to reflect truly changed lives. God will honor such a Bible-centered program, and the church may show truly amazing statistics, but comparison is difficult because the churches are operating on different frequencies. While one is interested in both quantity and quality, the other will resort to almost anything to get numerical results.

The context of Peter's epistle indicates that this revival trickery is the primary target of his attack—not the cultists or other Bible-denying infidels who are more easily distinguished as heretics.

THEIR FOLLOWING

> *And many shall follow their pernicious ways; by reason of whom the way of truth shall be evil spoken of (2:2).*

Unfortunately, false teachers gain large followings, not from paganism, but from within the church. Peter said *many* follow their immoral ways. Paul stated that *many* church members walk as enemies of the cross of Christ (Philippians 3:18).

In the Sermon on the Mount, the Lord said, "Many will say to me in that day, Lord, Lord, have we not prophesied in thy name? and in thy name have cast out devils? and in thy name done many wonderful works? And then will I profess unto them, I never knew you: depart from me, ye that work iniquity" (Matthew 7:22, 23).

Counterfeiting is the main work of Satan. Something of genuine value will always be imitated—God and Satan, Jesus Christ and the Antichrist, the Holy Spirit and the False Prophet. There is the true church, the bride of Christ, and there is the apostate church, the harlot. There are faithful men who for little gain and under much persecution preach the whole counsel of God, praying that He will bless with spiritual results. And, sure enough, there are those who, for personal profit and prestige, work out their own system of revival.

Any good thing is counterfeited, but cults and "works" religions are never counterfeited. They have no real value. In a sense, it is a great tribute to Biblical Christianity that there are so many imitations.

Why do people run to counterfeiters rather than to the true preachers of the Word? Peter said it was because of the fascination with the immoral lives of the teachers. Men always prefer darkness to light because their deeds are evil (John 3:19).

A genuine teacher must proclaim true discipleship. He will instruct his students to honor the Lord Jesus, forsake sin, and yield to God's will. On the other hand, the false teacher appeals with "walk the aisle" and "do your best," and the sinner thinks he has a ticket to Heaven.

Heresy peddlers gain a following because their shallow message gives license to sin rather than calling for self-denial. People love the immoral lives from which these teachings spring forth. It really helps soothe the conscience to have made a "religious decision."

This meaningless "salvation" blasphemes the way of truth so badly that the outside world fails to understand God's true way. Non-Christians continually sense this hypocrisy, and it drives them away from the truth which would save them. In fact, unbelievers often see through the sham and hypocrisy of our shallow methods more readily than "insiders" do.

False revivalism and flesh evangelism may well be the two biggest hindrances to reaching the lost. Both bring the Lord's work into disrepute.

THEIR MOTIVE

> *And through covetousness shall they with feigned words make merchandise of you: whose*

judgment now of a long time lingereth not, and their damnation [destruction] slumbereth not (2:3).

Peter not only exposed the heretical message of the false teachers, but he revealed their motives and mechanics. It is not surprising that these men are in church work to make money. Revivalism can be a good money-maker! Flesh evangelism pays well! Americans pay big prices to be entertained, and revival vaudevilles not only entertain but soothe guilty consciences.

For money's sake, slick-tongued sensationalists make a business of "converting" others. With feigned words they present an attractive salvation which costs nothing but a love offering—and eternal life!

God does not wink at such dangerous reprobates. He has already judged their motives and actions.

By way of contrast, it was a thrill to be associated with Doug, an Air Force pilot. This young Christian discovered his neighbor was seriously ill. Dave was an unlovely Jewish man who had traveled over the world writing pornographic novels. When Doug rushed him to the Chinese hospital for treatment, he was asked to sign a statement assuming full financial responsibility for Dave. This he did immediately.

Each day Doug faithfully visited Dave, telling him of the unsearchable riches of Christ, but receiving only harsh response. Dave's health grew worse, his hospital bill grew higher, and his mean temperament earned him the reputation of being the worst patient for whom the hospital had ever cared.

Then one day, as Doug and I visited him, there was a mighty change! Dave received the Lord Jesus as his Messiah!

After lingering, for some eighty days, Dave went to be with his Messiah. His memorial service in the hospital first were afraid to take care of this man, heard the gospel which had transformed him, and testified that indeed he was different from that day on!

What thrilling missionary work—but it cost Doug a large sum of money. Instead of complaining, he insisted on paying an extra four hundred dollars for funeral and burial expenses. When we tried to reimburse Doug from our church treasury, he refused, claiming this was the best money he had ever spent.

How embarrassing such self-giving dedication must be to those who are concerned only with making money from religious practices! A recent television news program showed the actual Form 1040 income tax statement of a well-known radio preacher. For the year his adjusted gross income was more than six million dollars. Certainly this is an extreme case, but it proves that big money can be made—if a person doesn't care about pleasing God or selling out the souls of men.

But our holy, righteous God must judge all sin; so Peter issued a solemn warning to false preachers and religious leaders. What a heavy price will be paid for filling churches with those who have not been born again!

THEIR DOOM

As proof that religious racketeers will not be spared, Peter presented three descriptions of God's past judgmental dealings. All false teachers face impending judgment with the same certainty and finality of these Old Testament examples.

God Spared Not the Angels That Sinned

> *For if God spared not the angels that sinned, but cast them down to hell, and delivered them into*

*chains of darkness, to be reserved unto judg-
ment (2:4).*

These angels, full of pride, supported Lucifer in his attempted rebellion against God. For this sin, God cast them into Tartarus, the pits of gloom in the deepest abyss of the netherworld, reserving them for the Great White Throne Judgment and eventual eternity in the Lake of Fire.

God Spared Not the Fallen World of the Pre-Flood Era

*And spared not the old world, but saved Noah the
eighth person, a preacher of righteousness, bringing in the flood upon the world of the ungodly (2:5).*

Disobedient sinners utterly disregarded Noah, God's preacher of righteousness. Imagine preaching the gospel for one hundred twenty years with only seven converts responding (and they were all from Noah's family)! Noah wouldn't be asked to preach in many churches if he were alive today, but he was God's man with God's message. And because people failed to heed him, God destroyed the whole civilization, except for Noah and his family. Apparently God is not as statistically minded as many of us!

God Spared Not Sodom and Gomorrha

*And turning the cities of Sodom and Gomorrha
into ashes condemned them with an overthrow,
making them an ensample [example] unto those
that after should live ungodly (2:6).*

These wicked cities, given over to fornication, homosexuality and other perversions, were reduced to ashes. America needs to learn from this object lesson. It has been said that if God doesn't punish the United States for her sexual sins He will have to apologize to Sodom and Gomorrha!

Almighty God spared not the proud angels, the entire world population of disobedient sinners, nor immoral cities. Peter pointed out that such a sin-hating God surely is able to reserve all false teachers for the awful day of judgment.

THEIR DELIVERANCE

Is there a way out for conniving men and their followers? Yes, for the God of love, who spared not the fallen angels, the corrupt world, and the sinful cities, also spared not one other person. "He that spared not his own Son, but delivered him up for us all, how shall he not with him also freely give us all things?" (Romans 8:32).

How this ought to break our hearts and show us His great displeasure with our sin! "For he hath made him to be sin for us, who knew no sin; that we might be made the righteousness of God in him" (II Corinthians 5:21). Christ died the sinner's death even though He is the only One who ever walked this earth without sinning. When He died, He "... bare our sins in his own body on the tree..." (I Peter 2:24).

He is the sinner's substitute. He died the sinner's death, and He was punished with the sinner's Hell. All the torments of Hell were poured out on Him in order to provide our way of escape. Sin must be punished and the believer's sin was punished in Christ. The cross, burial, and resurrection are God's way of delivering us from sin, judgment, Hell, false teachers, and false teachings.

What a great God we have! He saved Noah and his family from the flood because they repented, but His

deliverance of Lot shows even more clearly how He
delights in saving those who are unworthy.

> *And delivered just Lot, vexed with the filthy con-*
> *versation [manner of life] of the wicked. (For that*
> *righteous man dwelling among them, in seeing*
> *and hearing, vexed his righteous soul from day to*
> *day with their unlawful deeds) (2:7, 8).*

Lot's life stands in sharp contrast to that of Noah. Both
were believers and both were rescued by God before
judgment came. However, Noah was a preacher of
righteousness; Lot was a compromising, carnal backslider. The vile lives of the Sodomites tormented Lot and
wore him down, yet God had to force him to leave the
wicked city.

Later, in a drunken stupor, he fathered two sons by his
own daughters. Love of money and prestige caused him to
lose his property, his family, his influence on the perverse
city, and his touch with God. However, in the New
Testament, God refers to him as "justified" and
"righteous." Amazing grace! Lot was delivered out of
judgment because of his faith in God (verses 7, 8). The
worst of men can likewise be delivered when we heed
God's message.

> *The Lord knoweth how to deliver the godly out of*
> *temptations, and to reserve the unjust unto the*
> *day of judgment to be punished (2:9).*

God always removes the wheat before he burns the tares
(Matthew 13:30). He did not destroy the cities until Lot
was safely removed from the area. In like manner, He will
deliver all born-again children before He sends the
tribulation judgment. Many Christians entertain the
horrible idea that the church will go through the Great

chapel was a thrilling experience. Chinese nurses, who at Tribulation. This is inconsistent with the way God has always worked.

He has always punished the ungodly at His appointed time, but He first delivered His people out of these testings. The world is now facing its worst judgment, but before it comes, the Lord Jesus will return for His own (I Thessalonians 4:16-18). What a comforting promise for God's children!

There is no deliverance, however, for those outside the Lord Jesus. All who have not been born again have an appointment at the Great White Throne Judgment. An unbeliever may feel that he is special, that God understands he has a special problem, that somehow God will let him off, but this is not true. If you have rejected the Lord Jesus as your Saviour, God will reserve you (keep you in custody) until the day of judgment to see that you pay the full price for your sin.

The future is not bright for false church leaders who attempt to get rich, popular, or powerful at the expense of God's truth; nor is it bright for their followers.

THEIR CHARACTERISTICS: SPIRITUAL

How many times have you heard a sermon based upon II Peter 2:10-22? Most people would have to answer, "Never!" Seldom does anyone preach from these verses. One of the greatest theological libraries contains not a single sermon from this passage. Even works of noted expositors pass this section by in silence. Yet, it is such an important passage, for it pictures the life-styles and personalities of false religionists.

> *But chiefly them that walk after the flesh in the lust of uncleanness, and despise government. Presumptuous are they, self-willed, they are not*

> *afraid to speak evil of dignities. Whereas angels,*
> *which are greater in power and might, bring not*
> *railing accusation against them before the Lord*
> *(2:10, 11).*

Self-serving leaders walk in the old depraved sin nature. Their thought patterns are lustful and unclean. As their minds indulge in corrupt desires, their lives are filled with evil passions.

They despise authority. Unlike angels, who are greater in power and might, they are not afraid to speak against the governmental arrangements of God. Being concerned only about the "big I," they speak arrogantly against any Scripture which places others in authority over them. They refuse any role of submission because they are motivated by a desire to live for self. They make light of any unseen spiritual beings.

Fame and prestige are their goals. They want to be important, gratifying their sinful instincts and dispositions. Their only concern is themselves, and they will do anything to get what they want. To feather their nests, they will even preach the gospel, although they don't live by it.

> *But these, as natural brute beasts, made to be*
> *taken and destroyed, speak evil of the things that*
> *they understand not; and shall utterly perish in*
> *their own corruption (2:12).*

These men can prepare messages which appeal to guilty hearers, but they themselves are spiritually bankrupt, speaking evil of things they don't understand. They will be corrupted in their own corruption, facing the most severe punishment imaginable.

> *And shall receive the reward of unrighteousness,*

> *as they that count it pleasure to riot [revel] in the*
> *daytime. Spots they are and blemishes, sporting*
> *[reveling] themselves with their own deceivings*
> *while they feast with you (2:13).*

Collecting wages for doing wrong, they live in luxury and are lavishly entertained by their converts. They enjoy the soft life, reveling even in the daytime. They do not work for a living but live off the money they get from those they lead astray. Of course, they attend religious affairs, for appearance is important in sustaining their luxurious manner of life.

THEIR CHARACTERISTICS: MORAL

> *Having eyes full of adultery, and that cannot*
> *cease from sin; beguiling unstable souls; an heart*
> *they have exercised with covetous practices;*
> *cursed children (2:14).*

They are unable to stop sinning. These men entice their unsteady followers, often taking advantage of the high emotions which their flesh evangelism generates. They see in beautiful women the possibility of an adulterous relationship. Not only are they greedy for money, but they also covet another man's wife or daughter.

Because they are religious leaders, women trust them. They have a smooth way with words. An immoral person is dangerous whether he is armed with a pistol or a Bible.

Covetousness has become their permanent state. Their greedy lusts are illustrated in the life of the false prophet, Balaam:

> *Which have forsaken the right way, and are gone*
> *astray, following the way of Balaam the son of*

> *Bosor, who loved the wages of unrighteousness;*
> *But was rebuked for his iniquity: the dumb ass*
> *speaking with man's voice forbad the madness of*
> *the prophet (2:15, 16).*

Balaam was a believer who commercialized his gift and would do anything for money (Numbers 22:25, 31). Imagine being remembered in history only because he was covetous and taught Israel to sin! When he tried to curse Israel for financial gain, he was rebuked by a dumb donkey who, under God's control, had more sense than the erring prophet. Perhaps a plague of dumb donkeys would help our churches today!

THEIR CHARACTERISTICS: PRACTICAL

False revivalists are devoid of the Holy Spirit's power, and, as such, are of no value in the Lord's work. In fact, they do considerable harm, even though they may be popular in the highest religious circles:

> *These are wells without water, clouds that are*
> *carried with a tempest; to whom the mist of dark-*
> *ness is reserved forever (2:17).*

Such men can put on a good show and get statistical results, but they disappoint the thirsty as do dried up springs or clouds that bring no refreshing showers. Their ministries and messages are meaningless, containing no real spiritual substance.

Because they are impressive public speakers, they can stimulate the public with their eloquence and cleverness. They are especially dangerous to excited Christians who are just coming out of lethargy.

> *For when they speak great swelling words of*
> *vanity, they allure through the lusts of the flesh,*
> *through much wantonness, those that were clean*
> *escaped from them who live in error (2:18).*

False teachers can become famous. They may gain big
television or radio followings. Sometimes they are
honored by seminaries and universities. They may work
in the most prestigious churches or climb to the top in
denominational politics. But in God's sight, they are fakes
who use their natural talents to prey on the immature,
those who are just escaping error. Many times they use the
Bible only as a religious text; their real message is a
psychological appeal for a following.

A false teacher doesn't have much desire to get alone
with God and study the Scriptures. And it's best if his
followers don't learn too much, for a taste of thrilling
Bible truth might drive them to look elsewhere for
additional spiritual food!

My strongest conviction is that churches are suffering
most from a lack of verse-by-verse, expository Bible
teaching, the kind that shows people what the whole
counsel of God really is. Textual preaching in my opinion,
will never accomplish this.

> *While they promise them liberty, they themselves*
> *are the servants of corruption: for of whom a man*
> *is overcome, of the same is he brought in bond-*
> *age (2:19).*

Though they themselves are not free, they promise
freedom to their hearers. Because the teachers themselves
are in bondage to corruption, their promised freedom
often lasts only through the emotions of the meeting or
until the convert gets through the baptistry. From that
point on, there is often disillusionment with Christianity.

In response to her Sunday School teacher's question, "What is false doctrine?" a little girl answered, "False doctoring is when the doctor gives wrong medicine to the people who are sick and they die."

Perhaps this confused child furnished the best definition of false doctrine. It is wrong medicine. Many will learn too late that the Lord Jesus Christ and His shed blood are the only true remedies for sin.

THEIR CONVERTS

A question is raised as to whether those described in the next three verses are the deceivers or the deceived. The principles enunciated would pertain to either group; so this does not vitally affect the interpretation. It is likely, however, that the converts of false preachers are viewed here.

For if after they have escaped the pollutions of the world through the knowledge of the Lord and Saviour Jesus Christ, they are again entangled therein, and overcome, the latter end is worse with them than the beginning (2:20).

Here the King James Version contains an unfortunate translation. In the Greek manuscripts, there is no article *the* before *knowledge.* The reference is to *general* knowledge of Jesus Christ—exactly the kind that is imparted in shallow revivalism. The emotional decisions which follow often bring outward moral reformation for awhile. There is a surface experience but no new birth. There is emotional feeling but no change of will. Having no genuine spiritual substance to fall back on, the "converts" are in worse moral and spiritual shape than ever.

When false hope vanishes, a person tends to feel that he has "tried Christ, but it just didn't work." This, in turn, can lead to a complete moral collapse, and it becomes extremely difficult to reach that person with the true, life-transforming Bible message. Millions of people have been made immune to sound Bible teaching because they have been vaccinated with a small dose of "salvation."

> *For it had been better for them not to have known the way of righteousness, than, after they have known it, to turn from the holy commandment delivered unto them (2:21).*

6
The Common Denominator Of Spiritual Renewal

I do not mean to ridicule the work of any genuine pastor or evangelist who is seeking spiritual awakening. I want a God-honoring, world-shaking revival more than anything else in life. In fact, I do not regard revival as a luxury but as an absolute necessity, the only hope for our world until we see the Lord Jesus face to face.

My only intent is to show that real revival must initiate with God, not man. It must be God's production and carried on according to His guidelines. When we try to produce an awakening through a humanistic approach, we are only aiding God's enemies.

But when we practice His prescription for a rejuvenated faith—the stirring up by bringing people into remembrance of foundational Bible truths—we are guaranteed His results.

We have examined several concepts vital to the spiritual renewal of the defeated Christian. All of them are important. But if we were to boil them all down into one common element, we would discover that each is closely inter-related with a conscientious, open-hearted examination of the Word of God. There we find His principles, commands and promises for renewing close fellowship with Him, and for living the fulfilling life.

Throughout history, God has always initiated spiritual awakenings through the pages of His Word. On the Day of Pentecost, for example, God's people were filled with the Spirit, and three thousand souls were saved and added to the church. What brought about such amazing results? Was it Peter's powerful message on the death, burial, and resurrection of Jesus, or was it the ten-day prayer meeting in the upper room? Both factors contributed, but God's method of revival has always been to call people to remembrance of Bible truths — and sure enough, a "Bible conference" set the stage for this great awakening.

For forty days before the prayer meeting and the sermon, the resurrected Lord taught His apostles "of the things pertaining to the kingdom of God" (Acts 1:3c). "And beginning at Moses and all the prophets, he expounded unto them in all the scriptures the things concerning himself" (Luke 24:27). "And he said unto them, These are the words which I spake unto you, while I was yet with you, that all things must be fulfilled, which were written in the law of Moses, and in the prophets, and in the psalms, concerning me. Then opened he their understanding, that they might understand the scriptures" (Luke 24: 44, 45).

The apostles testified, as do all Bible-fed believers: "Did not our heart burn within us, while he talked with us by the way, and while he opened to us the scriptures?" (Luke 24:32b).

A forty-day Bible conference formed the basis for revival on the Day of Pentecost, and the Word was the key to victory throughout the revival—just as it is today!

Scanning the summary statements of the Book of Acts, we can also see that Bible conferences were instrumental in the success of the first-century churches. Each statement bears testimony to the power of the Word in bringing and sustaining revival.

In the church at Jerusalem: "And the word of God increased; and the number of the disciples multiplied in Jerusalem greatly; and a great company of the priests were obedient to the faith" (Acts 6:7). The growth of the church is described as an increase of the Word of God.

Evangelistic outreach prospered as the church grew through hearing and obeying the Word.

In Samaria and Africa: "Then had the churches rest throughout all Judaea and Galilee and Samaria, and were edified; and walking in the fear of the Lord, and in the comfort of the Holy Ghost [Spirit], were multiplied" (Acts 9:31). Orderly and continuous growth continued because the church was being built on a foundation of Bible study. "Therefore they that were scattered abroad went every where preaching the word" (Acts 8:4).

Philip first preached in Samaria, then later shared the Word with the Ethiopian. (The Word fostered foreign missions.) Stephen preached a Bible sermon that conquered the heart of the church's most active persecutor. The Word defeated the church's enemies. Everywhere, the Word brought the comfort of the Holy Spirit.

In Phoenicia, Cyprus, and Antioch in Syria: "But the Word of God grew and multiplied" (Acts 12:24). The tyrant Herod was eaten by worms and died, but God's Word which he had tried to suppress continued to grow and multiply. The Word is indestructible; it is settled forever in Heaven (Psalm 119:89).

Paul's First Missionary Journey: "And so were the churches established in the faith, and increased in number daily" (Acts 16:5). The Word was the main thrust of Paul's missionary work as he sought to establish churches.

Notice the importance given to the ministry of the Word:

> *And the next sabbath day came almost the whole city together to hear the word of God (Acts 13:44).*
> *And the word of the Lord was published throughout the region (Acts 13:49).*
> *Long time, therefore, abode they speaking boldly in the Lord, which gave testimony unto the word*

of his grace, and granted signs and wonders to be done by their hands (Acts 14:3).
Paul also and Barnabas continued in Antioch, teaching and preaching the word of the Lord, with many others also (Acts 15:35).

Paul's Second and Third Missionary Journeys: "So mightily grew the word of God and prevailed" (Acts 19:20). Revival fires spread everywhere. What were Paul's techniques? What gimmicks did he use? How did he build his crowds? How did he reach unbelievers?

In Philippi with the jailer: "And they spake unto him the word of the Lord, and to all that were in his house" (Acts 16:32).

In Thessalonica: "And Paul, as his manner was, went in unto them, and three sabbath days reasoned with them out of the scriptures" (Acts 17:2).

In Berea: "These were more noble than those in Thessalonica, in that they received the word with all readiness of mind, and searched the scriptures daily, whether those things were so" (Acts 17:11).

In Corinth: "And he continued there a year and six months, teaching the word of God among them" (Acts 18:11).

In Ephesus: "And this continued by [for] the space of two years; so that all they which dwelt in Asia heard the word of the Lord Jesus, both Jews and Greeks" (Acts 19:10).

This passage is not talking about people who lose their salvation. The God who promises everlasting life to born-again believers would lose His good name if that life did not last forever. The context indicates that those mentioned are the "converts" who were sold a bad bill of goods about salvation. Remember, they followed these false teachings because they liked the immoral ways of the teachers (verse 2), but they wanted these ways clothed in the respectability of religion.

In their quest for a soothed conscience, they gained a general knowledge of Jesus but rejected His terms of discipleship: "So likewise, whosoever he be of you that forsaketh not all that he hath, he cannot be my disciple" (Luke 14:33). With a full head-knowledge of Jesus, they reject the terms of God's offer for abundant and eternal life. They have tried to get to Heaven with a cheap religion that costs nothing.

All Christ-rejecters have their place reserved in Hell for all eternity; however, the Bible indicates that there are various degrees of punishment for unbelievers. The measuring rod seems to be "... unto whomsoever much is given, of him shall be much required ..." (Luke 12:48). Justice demands that the person who receives the greatest amount of scriptural light and has the choicest opportunities to receive the Lord Jesus will suffer more than the person with lesser light and opportunity.

The aisle-walking "baptized" church member who was not genuinely born again is worse off than the person who has had no real contact with Christianity. Hell at its best is no place to spend eternity, but unregenerated false teachers and their religious converts will get the very worst of it.

Peter declared that it would have been better for them to have never heard any of the Word preached. A superficial contact with the Word can bring a hardened condition, along with greater condemnation. A little knowledge truly is dangerous.

> *But it is happened unto them according to the true proverb, The dog is turned to his own vomit again; and the sow that was washed to her wallowing in the mire (2:22).*

Often this verse is used to demonstrate that a person can lose his salvation; however, nothing indicates that the converts referred to ever possessed salvation. They are victims of those who teach for their own profit. These proverbs deal with the matter of outward moral reformation.

In mentioning the dog, Peter quotes from Proverbs 26:11. The second saying was a pagan proverb, not found in the Scriptures. Both stress that we go the way of our inner nature. Therefore, if the nature of a sinner is not changed, he will return to the old paths of sin. Outward reformation will last only a brief period if the heart is not changed. As a dog returns to his vomit and the sow to its filth, so will one turn back to the way of sin if he has never truly been redeemed.

Most of us are familiar with the story of the prodigal son, but Dr. J. Vernon McGee tells a fascinating story of the prodigal pig, based on the proverb of the sow that was washed and returned to her wallowing.

The little pig became sold on religion and said to the prodigal son, "You've made your father's house sound so attractive! I don't know about the clean sheets on the bed, and I don't know about a clean linen tablecloth, but I'll try it. I'll go along with you if you don't mind."

So the pig went with the prodigal son to the father's house. However, the pig didn't last there as long as the son had lasted in the pigpen. One day he said, "Prodigal son, I'm not happy here; I don't like those white sheets on the bed. And I don't know why we have to go to the table and why everyone has to put his dinner on his own plate. Couldn't we just have a trough and all of us jump in and have a lot of fun?"

The prodigal son replied, "When you're the son of the father, you have his nature, and you like things white and clean. You might get in a pigpen like I did, but you won't stay in the pigpen."

"Well," the little pig said, "I was born there, and I like it, and I know where my father is, and I'm going back to my father's house."

When he got back, he saw his old man lying in a loblolly, and he squealed and made a jump for him and was never so happy in all his life.

It's confusing when pigs go into the Father's house, and the sons go into the pigpen. However, if you wait long enough, the sons will go home, and the pigs will return to the pigpen!

Likewise, unless the inner nature is changed, sinners will always prefer the pigpen of sin to the Father's house. While they may "visit" the Father for awhile, the unconverted will always find their way back to wallowing in the mire.

Spurgeon said, "If that dog or sow had been born again and had received the nature of a sheep, it never would have gone back to the filth depicted here." This is why the Lord Jesus stresses: "You must be born again." We need a brand new nature to become Christians and to please God.

We would do well to follow Paul's admonition: "Examine yourselves, whether ye be in the faith; prove your own selves. Know ye not your own selves, how that Jesus Christ is in you, except [unless] ye be reprobates [discredited]?" (II Corinthians 13:5).

Flesh evangelism not only doesn't save you, but it drives you farther from the Lord. It is not enough to "walk the aisle"; it is not enough to be baptized and join the church; it is not enough to let your emotions get stirred in a religious gathering. It *is* enough to be born again, for then the Lord Jesus dwells in you and you receive a new nature. Christ in you is your hope of glory—and glory's only hope!

Two types of teachers make their appeal to men: the false and the true. Those who choose to follow the anti-Biblical teacher will suffer the fate of the false. Those who choose to follow the godly will share in the pleasures and joys of the true. The godly believer is secure forever in

Jesus Christ.

Do you know the Bible well enough to detect the false teacher? Using the Word as your standard, can you see beyond good looks, rich talent, clever techniques, high office, TV or radio success, or other externals to the real message of God?

The Berean people were specially commended by Paul because they daily checked his message to be sure he preached the truth. "These were more noble than those in Thessalonica, in that they received the word with all readiness of mind, and searched the scriptures daily, whether those things were so" (Acts 17:11). There is no other way to expose the devil's disciples and defeat false revivalism.

Paul's Imprisonment in Rome: "And Paul dwelt two whole years in his own hired house, and received all that came in unto him, Preaching the kingdom of God, and teaching those things which concern the Lord Jesus Christ, with all confidence, no man forbidding him" (Acts 28:30, 31).

Paul's lifework ended in triumph. In spite of hatred and opposition, he continued to proclaim the Word. To those outside the prison he proclaimed the kingdom. To those inside he taught about the Lord Jesus.

The effectiveness of first-century Christianity grew out of the ministry of the Word. We dare not minimize the power of the Word of God in changing the lives of people, churches, and nations today.

Since Bible days, God has continued to intervene in the affairs of men with great awakenings. In each instance, world-transforming revival fires spread as the Word of God was taught. The plan of salvation, marvelous as it is, was not enough; the whole counsel of God had to be proclaimed.

Most God-blessed revivals of the past would correspond more favorably with today's "Bible conferences" than with what we term "revival." The methods and messages of Paul, Savonarola, Luther, Whitefield, and Edwards would be difficult to compare with those used in revival efforts today. More than anything else, people need to know what to do with this great salvation after they receive it. The foundational truths which Peter calls to our remembrance furnish the answer.

Even the Old Testament revivals were stimulated by reading and expounding on the Word. Dr. C. E. Autrey, in *Revivals of the Old Testament,* shared several excellent revival lessons for our generation.

> Most of the Old Testament revivals were stimulated by reading and expounding the law and by a return to God's commandments and precepts. The text for the Mount Carmel revival was Deuteronomy 11:17. The revival under Hezekiah was promoted and inspired around the ritual of Leviticus and Deuteronomy. The revival in Josiah's time came from the rediscovery of the book of the law.
>
> The post-captivity revival was born when Ezra read the law from a wooden pulpit in the streets of Jerusalem and the Levites expounded it to the whole congregation. These great revivals of the Old Testament constitute some of our most precious treasures of revival history.

Everything revival-minded Christians are searching for today can be found in revivals of the past—in Old Testament days, New Testament days, and throughout church history. Various conditions prevailed, different techniques were used, but always the plan which Peter gave us—a spiritual stirring resulting from remembrance of God's foundational truths—is the common denominator of genuine spiritual awakenings.

7
How To Survive
Future Shock

*I*n II Peter 3, Peter reaffirms his purpose for writing: To wake up and revive believers through calling to remembrance the foundational truths of God.

> *This second epistle, beloved, I now write unto you; in both which I stir up your pure minds by way of remembrance (3:1).*

Chapter 1 emphasized that spiritual renewal comes from appropriating all the blessings of Christ to our lives. Now Peter selects one outstanding revival truth and emphasizes it with four exhortations. He shows that a truly revived Christian must have a vital hope in the sure and sudden return of the Lord. He is coming again, and Peter wants that blessed hope, which burns so dimly in the lives of many, to be fanned into a lively flame. The return of the Lord is an essential theme of the rejuvenated faith.

The structure of this chapter is fascinating. It is a preacher's delight, for it contains a built-in sermon outline. Each exhortation is addressed to the "beloved."

> Beloved . . . be mindful (3:1, 2).
> Beloved . . . be not ignorant (3:8).
> Beloved . . . be diligent (3:14).
> Beloved . . . beware (3:17).

The term *beloved* is rich! It is really a title for the Lord

Jesus Christ. On several occasions, God looked down from Heaven upon Jesus and said, "This is my beloved Son in whom I am well pleased." God has not been pleased with His world since Adam and Eve plunged it into sin.

A study of the Scriptures shows that after sin marred His creation, God never again expressed pleasure with anything or anyone except his Son and those in whom He lives and works.

You and I are no exceptions. God cannot be pleased with us. Try as hard as we can, there is no way to commend ourselves to Him. Joining church, being baptized, trying to live a good life—it doesn't matter how sincere our efforts, sinful man just can't please Holy God! He cannot accept us as we are.

Only His beloved Son pleases Him; so it is imperative that His beloved Son dwell in us. This is what Christianity is—Christ in you, the hope of glory (Colossians 1:27).

We can't be accepted on our own, but we can be "... accepted in the beloved. In whom we have redemption through his blood, the forgiveness of sins, according to the riches of his grace" (Ephesians 1:6, 7). God accepts us if He sees His Son living in us. We are not accepted if He sees us living our own lives, no matter how religious we may be, or how far our religious pedigree might extend.

When Betty, the scrubwoman, gave her life to Christ, an infidel who worked with her continually gave her a hard time about her newfound faith.

He said, "Betty, I hear you got religion. What's it like to be a saint?"

Now Betty admittedly was not a scholar, and questions like this confused her. She was just joyous that she was saved and on the way to Heaven. But when the man persisted with, "How does it feel to be a Christian?" Betty gave a classic answer.

"Well, I don't know much about it. It just feels, though,

like I'm standing in the Lord's shoes, and He's standing in mine."

Betty was implying that she was "accepted in the beloved." Nineteen hundred years ago, the Lord Jesus stood in our shoes at Calvary and was punished for our sin. Today we live the successful life when we let Christ stand in our shoes through the process of swapping out. What a thrill it is to be God's child and to be addressed as "beloved."

Is this epistle addressed to you? Can you say with Paul, "Christ lives in me"? If so, these four commands concerning His future return should be taken seriously. They will renew you and equip you to live abundantly.

BELOVED, BE MINDFUL

First, be mindful of what the true prophets say:

That ye may be mindful of the words which were spoken before by the holy prophets, and of the commandment of us the apostles of the Lord and Saviour (3:2).

After concluding his long warning about false teachers, Peter contrasted them with the true prophets and apostles. While there are many counterfeit revivalists, there are also many true men of God who are characterized by strong belief in the Book, the Blood, and the Blessed Hope! We should be aware of what they say.

Next, be mindful of a special group of false teachers:

Knowing this first, that there shall come in the last days scoffers, walking after their own lusts, And saying, Where is the promise of his coming? for since the fathers fell asleep, all things con-

> *tinue as they were from the beginning of the*
> *creation (3:3, 4).*

In the last days, the period prior to the Lord's return, we can expect particularly ungodly influence from a group called "scoffers." These religious men ridicule the glorious truth of the return of the Lord Jesus by asking, "Where is the promise of His coming?" They attempt to discredit God's Word by saying, "It has been almost two thousand years since Christ promised to return. This lapse of time shows that God does not keep His word." Such false teaching tends to make Christians lethargic instead of alert.

Scoffers also teach that everything has remained the same since the world was created, that God has never intervened in the affairs of men. They reason that there has never been any cataclysmic change in the world since its creation.

Not only are these scoffers poor theologians, but they need refresher courses in world history. They have forgotten that a universal flood covered the earth, destroying the physical world and the creatures living in it. What a cataclysmic change this judgment brought in the course of human events! The reality of the flood testifies to the falsity of the scoffers' position.

> *For this they willingly are ignorant of, that by the*
> *word of God the heavens were of old, and the*
> *earth standing out of the water and in the water:*
> *Whereby the world that then was, being over-*
> *flowed with water, perished: But the heavens and*
> *the earth, which are now, by the same word are*
> *kept in store, reserved unto fire against the day of*
> *judgment and perdition of ungodly men (3:5-7).*

Peter exposed the self-styled intelligentsia as ignorant!

And they are willingly ignorant! They keep on ignoring the truth because they are not ready for the Lord's return. They are "walking after their own lusts" (verse 3). They crave prestige, power, material goods, and indulgence in things of the flesh. To see the Lord Jesus is the last thing they want! This would be a source of total embarrassment to them; so they live in willful ignorance of His coming, pretending it won't happen. They do not believe in His return simply because they do not want Him to come back!

The same attitude can be seen in those who call themselves atheists. Romans 1 reveals that everyone on earth, including atheists, knows of the Creator God but walks away from Him because of sin. An atheist is so steeped in sin that he *wishes* there were no God. In like manner, a scoffer is so involved with himself that he *wishes* the Lord Jesus weren't coming back to judge the sins of the world.

Notice that Peter said these scoffers are willingly ignorant of the word of God (verse 5). He related three activities of God's word which make this ignorance evident.

First, creation of the world was by the word of God (verse 5). While many scholars have tried to explain creation, the Bible gives the simplest, easiest-to-believe description. Creation came by the spoken word of God. Each of the six days of creation activity begins with the phrase, "and God said." God simply spoke this world and all mankind into existence. His word is all-powerful.

It is amusing (although a bit sickening) to watch well-educated people doing their best to include monkeys, apes, and amoebae in their family tree. I go to the zoo to visit animals, not to see my ancestors! No doubt there were some bad actors on my family tree, but they were all people, right back to Adam. Some of them may have hung by their necks, but none of them hung by their tails! How foolish to reject the simple Bible fact of creation! God spoke everything into being. We were created by His word.

There has never been a scientific, geological, or archeological discovery which contradicts the Word of God, and there never will be. Theory after theory of man's is laid aside as untenable, but the Word of God remains settled forever. What a good reason for knowing the future of the earth as God records it!

Second, the flood came by the word of God (3:6). Peter noted that God once destroyed a generation of scoffers. When sin caused extreme violence and corruption in the human race, the word of the Holy Creator brought about the promised judgment. He spoke, and the flood came, an activity of His word. The result certainly proves that all things have not continued in the same unchanging course throughout history.

Third, destruction of the world will be by the word of God (3:7). Things will not always continue as they are. One day in the future, the God who spoke this world into existence will speak again to destroy it. The Lord Jesus is waiting only for the word of God before He comes to remove His people from this impending judgment. One of these days, perhaps sooner than we think, all scoffers will be silenced. Once the world was destroyed by flood; the next destruction will be by fire!

BELOVED . . . BE NOT IGNORANT

Ignorance causes believers to succumb to the wicked teachings of scoffers. We need to be enlightened as to why the Lord has not yet returned. Two reasons are presented.

First, the clock of Heaven is not the clock of earth:

> *But, beloved, be not ignorant of this one thing, that one day is with the Lord as a thousand years, and a thousand years as one day (3:8).*

God does not look on time as we do. In fact, He doesn't own a watch, and in Heaven we won't need those things either! Have you ever realized what a slave you are to time? That slavery will be missing in eternity.

One special blessing we'll have in Heaven that we should have now is sufficient "time" to worship. People make time for just about everything else, but a worship service must not be too long!

I never understood my seminary professors taking one hour a day, four days a week, to instruct me not to go more than twenty minutes a sermon. Not much Bible truth can be taught in a twenty-minute sermonette, and this is probably why we have so many Christianettes. We will discover too late just how much blessing we have missed by not allowing God ample time to work, both in worship services and in daily activities.

If we take verse 8 literally, two days have not yet passed in God's mind since Jesus promised to come again. Augustine said, "God is patient because he is eternal. He takes his time because all time is his. There are a thousand years within his day." The basic teaching, however, is that a promise of God made thousands of years ago is just as valid today as the day it was made.

The second reason that the Lord has not yet returned is that God longs for the salvation of souls:

> *The Lord is not slack concerning his promise, as some men count slackness, but is longsuffering to us-ward, not willing that any should perish, but that all should come to repentance (3:9).*

God is not one day off schedule. He is not slow or negligent concerning His promise. He permits time to continue because of His faithfulness in saving souls. Judgment is delayed because of extraordinary patience in bringing in His elect. He is preparing His bride, the church, before He sends the Bridegroom. He is waiting for the entire body to be complete.

Someday, somewhere, that last lost soul will be saved, and the Lord Jesus will come for His own. What a gracious purpose in His delay! It shows His deep concern for the lost and gives further opportunity for people to prepare for His coming.

This does not teach that all men everywhere will be saved. God will complete His church before the coming judgment, but every human being who rejects the Lord Jesus will face that judgment.

One preacher pictured God saying, "Jesus, go for your bride." But Jesus is standing in the doorway, holding the door open, saying, "Not yet, Father, there are a few more who will come in."

While this illustration has theological shortcomings, it does indicate how the Lord will return when all His elect come to repentance.

THE FUTURE CATASTROPHE

Ever since the sad story of Genesis 3, the earth has been under the righteous curse of God. The worst is yet in store, for the Lord has promised exceedingly fearful consequences to those who reject His mercy and love.

But the day of the Lord will come as a thief in the night; in the which the heavens shall pass away with a great noise, and the elements shall melt with fervent heat, the earth also and the works that are therein shall be burned up (3:10).

Three phenomena are mentioned in this passage. First, there will be a great noise. The word used here speaks of "a great rushing sound like a fierce flame violently whipped by a strong wind." It might well refer to the terrible noise which accompanies atomic explosions.

Second, there are "elements," a reference to "the first thing from which other things result." The basic material of creation is the atom, and the world as we know it is an accumulation of atoms.

Third, there is "fervent heat," so fierce that it melts the elements (atoms). The entire universe is constructed so that a tremendous release of energy will accompany its destruction.

Although Peter never heard of atomic explosions, it seems likely that God will use such to bring an end to the sin-contaminated earth. Peter, of course, knew nothing about the heat and energy captured in the atom, but the Holy Spirit moved upon him in such a way that he could accurately record God's message of the future—another proof of the inspiration of the Scriptures.

While we cannot say dogmatically that the destruction of the earth will come through an atomic blast, our knowledge of atomic energy makes this passage less mysterious than it was fifty years ago. One thing is certain. Man will not destroy himself although he seems bent on doing so. When the time comes, God will destroy the earth as He has promised. He is truly in charge of this world. He can predict the future because He controls the future.

And so, the time is coming when the present universe will be destroyed. Elements and heavenly bodies will be scorched and dissolved. As the earth disintegrates into flames, all man's works will be burned up. Everything that man has constructed—architectural miracles, works of art, magnificent sports arenas, cultural centers, and dens of iniquity—will fall in one common crash. Whole cities, mountains, and forests will dissolve. Solid portions of the earth will be liquefied.

With one act, God will destroy every last trace of sin on earth. Gone will be our homes, cars, boats, sports equipment, works of art, bank accounts—everything we own. Truly there is no such thing as material security! Only the Word of God will stand! The Lord Jesus said, "Heaven and earth shall pass away, but my words shall not pass away" (Matthew 24:35).

When will this destruction take place? We do not know the day or times or season, and we should not waste any time trying to determine God's schedule. Jesus said, "But of that day and hour knoweth no man, no, not the angels of heaven, but my Father only" (Matthew 24:36). The Day of the Lord will come as suddenly as a thief in the night.

The term *Day of the Lord* refers to an extended period of judgment, beginning with the coming tribulation period and concluding with the destruction of the heavens and earth and the Great White Throne Judgment. In this period, God will abolish sin and wickedness.

Although this day will overtake many as a thief in the night, it need not overtake us. Hundreds of Bible prophecies concerning future events point to the same general warning: "Therefore be ye also ready: for in such an hour as ye think not the Son of man cometh" (Matthew 24:44). God promises to remove us from this planet before He turns the atoms loose on it. We will watch this scene of destruction from the Heavenly City, thanking God that through His grace, love, and mercy we have escaped.

The rapture is the next scheduled event on God's prophetic calendar. Although this term is not found in the Scriptures, the teaching that the Lord will come for His true church is stressed throughout the New Testament. We do not look for wrath but for rapture! Born-again ones don't need to be looking for bombs falling from Heaven; rather for the Lord Jesus to come in the clouds. What blessed hope! Paul declared that we ". . . wait for his Son from heaven, whom he raised from the dead, even Jesus, which delivered us from the wrath to come" (I Thessalonians 1:10).

HOW TO PREPARE FOR THE FUTURE

> *Seeing then that all these things shall be dis-*
> *solved, what manner of persons ought ye to be in*
> *all holy conversation [living] and godliness (3:11).*

These inevitable facts of the future should make a serious and important impact on the lives of all believers. The Scriptures associate hope with holiness. This explains why Peter includes prophetic teachings in his plans for revival. The teaching of Christ's coming is a present incentive to holiness of life and wholeheartedness in service. Such a truth must affect the believer's character and behavior, and that is exactly what brings revival.

Of course, no revival power is derived from *arguing* about His return, nor is there any spiritual value for those who curiously indulge only in the spectacularism of the future. But he who momentarily expects his Lord's return will walk in purity, godliness, and integrity; then his life will have an impact on the world of unbelievers.

Peter lists several characteristics of a Christian whose life is influenced by the practical hope of Christ's return. First, there is holy conduct. Both our outward behavior and our inward character should reflect the indwelling Christ. Remember that we do not produce such behavior. Both holy living and godly character result from allowing the Lord Jesus to live out His life in and through us. God has given us all things that pertain to life and godliness (1:3). Belief in His sure and sudden return inspires us to partake of the necessary resources for holy conduct.

Belief in the second coming not only affects what we are but what we do. It leads to a special assignment:

> *Looking for and hasting unto the coming of the*
> *day of God, wherein the heavens being on fire*

shall be dissolved, and the elements shall melt with fervent heat (3:12).

The Day of God, distinct from the Day of the Lord, is a period of time which refers to eternity future. As the destruction in the judgmental Day of the Lord comes to an end, this wonderful Day of God is ushered in. Every spiritual person is keenly anticipating this time, and such a watchful attitude has a marked effect upon daily living.

Hasting or *hastening* means "urging on," having an earnest desire for the Day of God. By preaching the gospel and seeking the salvation of lost souls, we can actually hasten the day when the Lord comes for His church and begins the chain of events which bring in eternity. In verse 9 we learned that the Lord has delayed His coming until His bride is complete. It is every Christian's duty and privilege to share the faith so that the body of Christ will be complete.

When that last soul is reached, the Lord Jesus will come for us. We can hasten that day by reaching the lost with the message of salvation.

When I was a young Christian, a friend admonished me to "Keep looking up; Jesus is coming!" What excellent advice! It's an excellent incentive for holy living. Paul wrote that ". . . denying ungodliness and worldly lusts, we should live soberly, righteously, and godly, in this present world; Looking for that blessed hope, and the glorious appearing of the great God and our Saviour Jesus Christ" (Titus 2:12, 13). Every Christian ought to be looking up, waiting for Christ's return with keen anticipation.

I was a bit perplexed a few years ago when another friend said, "Jesus is coming; keep looking down!" After looking up for so many years, I was inclined to disregard this new advice as heresy. However, my friend explained that, because the Lord's coming is imminent, we should be looking out on the fields which are white unto harvest. We should be deeply concerned about serving others with a view to helping them prepare to meet the Lord.

Both friends were right. We should be looking up, watching with eyes of faith for His coming, and we should be looking down, working in the power of the Holy Spirit to reach others, hastening the day of His return.

> *Nevertheless we, according to his promise, look for new heavens and a new earth, wherein dwelleth righteousness (3:13).*

The word *nevertheless* is significant. The preceding verses show the terrifying picture of everything going up in smoke with the whole earth being dissolved by fire, but the word *nevertheless* indicates that this is not the future for those who are born again. By contrast, we have something much better in view—a universe which portrays the righteousness of God. The future is extremely bright for those who are in Christ Jesus. In the final phase of this earth, righteousness will be permanently at home.

Christians are not bound to this earth. We should not strive to accumulate what must soon be destroyed. When we compare the characteristics of this age with the coming righteous, peaceful world, we readily see the wisdom of the Lord's words, "Lay not up for yourselves treasures upon earth, where moth and rust doth corrupt, and where thieves break through and steal: But lay up for yourselves treasures in heaven" (Matthew 6:19, 20a).

BELOVED . . . BE DILIGENT

> *Wherefore, beloved, seeing that ye look for such things, be diligent that ye may be found of him in peace, without spot, and blameless (3:14).*

Again and again, the emphasis on holiness is repeated in the Scriptures. In God's renewal plan, He is primarily concerned about what kind of people we are. Often our revival programs emphasize only schedule-chasing activism; a high premium is placed on what we can get people to do. But most of us need to beware the barrenness of a busy life. Great spiritual victory will always come to the individual or church when priority is placed on character building, and the lost will come to know our Lord Jesus when they see what He is doing in and through us.

Peter stressed this priority on holy living in his first epistle. He said, "But ye are a chosen generation, a royal priesthood, an holy nation, a peculiar [special] people [Note: this is what you *are*]; that ye should shew forth the praises of him who hath called you out of darkness into his marvellous light [Note: this is what you *do*]" (I Peter 2:9).

Peter was not the only one to stress this approach to revival victory. David testified, "I waited patiently for the Lord; and he inclined unto me, and heard my cry. He brought me up also out of an horrible pit, out of the miry clay, and set my feet upon a rock, and established my goings. And he hath put a new song in my mouth, even praise unto our God" (Psalm 40:1-3a).

David stated that he was saved, secure, singing, and serving because of the Lord's work in his life. The result? "Many shall see it, and fear, and shall trust in the Lord" (Psalm 40:3b).

Paul, in telling of the great value of preaching the word, said, "But if all prophesy, and there come in [to a public meeting] one that believeth not, or one unlearned, he is convinced [convicted] of all, he is judged of all. And thus are the secrets of his heart made manifest; and so falling down on his face he will worship God and *report that God is in you of a truth*" (I Corinthians 14:24, 25, italics mine).

What makes the unbeliever fall on his face and worship

God? It is the sight of God dwelling in Christians. We believers earn the right to witness when we show what a difference Christ has made in our character and behavior. A true witness has a much greater responsibility than going out on Thursday night church visitation or merely asking people if they are saved. Our first responsibility is to let the indwelling Christ transform our lives. This kind of evangelism produces fruit that lasts.

Dennis responded to a gospel invitation one evening. He said, "I've come to Christ because I've been watching my sergeant over there for the past few months. I've seen Christ change his life and make him into the best boss on the base." He pointed to a quiet, shy sergeant who had just been saved a few months before. Al was not a noisy, boisterous soul-winner, but in his quiet manner he was quick to share the hope that was in him with the men who worked with him. What a thrilling way to reach the lost!

One day I was introduced to a sin-hardened old sergeant whose life was being wasted. The door was opened for me to share the Lord with him when he said, "I don't know what's going on down at that church, but I want to thank you for turning my two biggest goof-offs into my two best workers." This is the kind of witness program the Bible calls for, and it surely makes a pastor's heart flutter!

The Christian who is anxiously awaiting the return of the Lord will make every effort to be found in peace, without spot, and blameless. This threefold description of the prepared believer is possible because we have His life in us. "Not I, but Christ lives in me" was Paul's secret of Christian success, and it is *our* only hope.

Conditions on earth are going to grow steadily worse, but in this desperately dark, sin-stricken world, the believer finds encouragement and hope in the fact that his Sovereign God is on the throne. We are fully confident that He will soon step down and right all wrongs. This is our incentive for a life of peace and assurance. Daily

anticipation of our Lord's return inspires us to live lives
that are wellpleasing to Him, to be quiet and confident in
the midst of this world's confusion and chaos, and to
reach out for the salvation of others.

> *And account that the longsuffering of our Lord*
> *is salvation; even as our beloved brother Paul*
> *also according to the wisdom given unto him*
> *hath written unto you (3:15).*

After proper priority has been placed on showing a life
of peace and victory, Peter stresses the need to share with
others the salvation message. Showing the Christ-life is
necessary, but it isn't everything. We must show and *tell!*

To tell without showing is hypocrisy which the
unbeliever can always read.

To show without telling is stealing the Lord's glory.

If He gives us the victory, He deserves all the credit, and
we must tell others what He has done for us. Otherwise,
those who observe our behavior will give us undeserved
credit, and we will be stealing glory that is rightfully His.

The psalmist said, "Let the redeemed of the Lord say so,
whom he hath redeemed from the hand of the enemy"
(Psalm 107:2). Every redeemed child of God should be
most happy to tell of the victory he is enjoying.

Peter mentioned again that we should be grateful for
each day the Lord delays His coming since this provides
additional time for procrastinators to be added to His
body. We should hope that He comes today, but if He
doesn't, the added time should be used to show our
concern and to share our faith with those who are not yet
prepared.

> *As also in all his epistles, speaking in them of*
> *these things, in which are some things hard to be*
> *understood, which they that are unlearned and*
> *unstable wrest, as they do also the other scrip-*

tures, unto their own destruction (3:16).

Peter recommended Paul's epistles because of the deep insight into spiritual truths they furnish. Paul's writings are not all easy to understand, but Peter does not mean that they cannot be understood. The Holy Spirit can give enlightenment and illumination to make the meaning clear. It is only men who are without the Spirit and live by their own emotions who will twist and distort these Scriptures to their own ruin.

BELOVED . . . BEWARE

Ye therefore, beloved, seeing ye know these things before, beware lest ye also, being led away with the error of the wicked, fall from your own stedfastness (3:17).

Here is the final reference to "these things"—our seven traits of a growing life—which Peter has stressed as the essentials for defeating spiritual lethargy. Since the recipients of this epistle had previous knowledge of God's revival plan, they were without excuse for living in defeat. Now, God's people have had this epistle for almost two thousand years, and there is no reason for the abuses and errors which prevail in our revival and evangelistic efforts. God will not hold us guiltless when we resort to crowd-pleasing, man-made strategies rather than calling people to remembrance of these things.

The "error of the wicked" is ignoring God's Word. He has provided the message, the methods, and the means to bring about powerful revival. Such renewal will come when we consult His instruction manual and provide His message by using His methods.

But grow in grace, and in the knowledge of our

126

Lord and Saviour, Jesus Christ. To him be glory
both now and for ever. Amen (3:18).

Growth in grace and knowledge of our Lord and Saviour
is the prime requirement of spiritual vitality. Since
growth is the main business of life, it is not strange that
the apostle should close with this admonition.

To grow in grace is to become increasingly conscious of
our moment-by-moment dependence upon the indwelling
Spirit of the living Christ. Of course, the starting point for
this abundant life is to be born again, for there can be no
growth if there is no life. Dead things simply do not grow.
After we receive the new life of Christ, the process of
growth must begin. Peter tells exactly how this growth
begins: "As newborn babes, desire the sincere [pure] milk
of the word, that ye may grow thereby: If so be ye have
tasted that the Lord is gracious" (I Peter 2:2, 3).

Unfortunately, many Christians never get past the
birth stage. While they rejoice in their ticket to Heaven,
they have no vital relationship with the indwelling
Christ. They attempt to rejoice in thoughts of eternity, but
this present life is empty and purposeless because the
Lord is not real or precious. As it concerns practical living,
He could be on vacation and never be missed! Such self-
living Christians are hindrances to renewal and barriers
to blessing, regardless of their church record.

The answer to such spiritual dilemma is to secure
knowledge of the Lord Jesus Christ and to translate it into
life. There is nothing so attractive as the person who is
being conformed to His glorious image. There is nothing
so thrilling as allowing Him to live in us. The translation
from carnality to spirituality is real revival victory.

As has been said, the knowledge necessary to do this
comes from only one source, the Bible! It is absolutely
impossible to know Him apart from the Word. Bible study
is not a luxury; it is an imperative. It is our spiritual food,

and without food there can be no growth.

F. B. Meyer said, "We can measure our growth in grace by the growth of our love for private Bible study."

Pity the poor Christian who does not have a time of personal devotions in which he gets better acquainted with his Saviour. Such a man is denying himself the opportunity to grow and glow. He is shutting out all spiritual blessing from his life, and he can pass on only spiritual defeat to others, no matter how sincerely he tries.

The message is clear to each of us. Nothing can displace the importance of a regular, openhearted study of, and meditation on, God's Word. As individuals, God speaks to us as we get alone with Him. In group settings, He not only meets individual needs, but those of the whole body of believers as they examine and apply the Scriptures together.

From God's Word, we learn and reinforce the principle of "swapping out" our weakness and sin for His strength and purity. Of letting Him live the Christian life in and through us. Of letting Him fill us with His supernatural love, joy, and peace, as—through prayer—we yield to His leading moment by moment.

Jesus is the same yesterday, today, and forever. His ways are unchanging. They are as effective and powerful today as they were in Peter's day. If we are to experience a genuine spiritual awakening, these eternal ways must be made operative in our individual lives.

It is not enough to call a nation or a denomination or even a church to revival. Revival must always begin within the individual.

It can begin in you if you are willing to let the Lord Jesus Christ become your life.

That's the simple, yet dynamic key to beating those spiritual blahs . . . and living life the way God meant it to be!